THE REALM OF ART

THE REALM OF ART

John M. Anderson

1967

THE PENNSYLVANIA STATE UNIVERSITY PRESS

UNIVERSITY PARK AND LONDON

Library of Congress Catalog Card Number 67–16195
Copyright © 1967 by The Pennsylvania State University
All rights reserved
Printed in the United States of America

Designed by Glenn Ruby

to Gale

PREFACE

Many people like to think about things and to reflect on their significance. I imagine it is fair to say that this is one of my characteristics and also, I expect, that of anyone who reads the following account of the name and nature of art. Yet my efforts in writing this account were only incidentally intended to satisfy this tendency to thoughtfulness; and I hope that my readers will discover, as they read on, other reasons for continuing.

Let me anticipate. I have tried to discuss a number of pivotal issues in art, such as the place of truth there, the nature of tragedy, the character of beauty, and the quality of the sublime. In order to understand art and to reflect upon it to some purpose one needs to be aware of these areas of crisis, and something of the reasons why there is a basic issue in respect to each of them. I have directed my discussion to this end. In addition, I have illustrated this discussion with specific examples, partly because the interpretation of examples is the best way to show the provocativeness of taking a stand in respect to these issues, and partly in order to make it quite clear that I am taking a stand.

This provocativeness is a means of expressing the novelty of insight and perspective which I hope to offer on art in general, and on various aspects of it in particular. Such expression, I believe, is important in itself. However, taking a stand is also a device for expressing my interest in the philosophy of art, which is something quite different from thinking about and reflecting upon art. Indeed, it is only fair to note in advance that my interest in the philosophy of art, that is, in philosophy, is central to all that I have to say. Those readers who are not consciously or unconsciously committed to philosophy may find that the drift of the discussion occasionally leads into strange and uncongenial realms. To some extent such readers may back water when this drift becomes too strong, or skip a few pages in order to remain out of the current. Still, I would hardly expect anyone to whom philosophy is really uncongenial to respond favorably to the pressures of my discussion.

I mean to suggest that while this discussion of the name and nature of art may satisfy a variety of interests, it does comprise an introduction to philosophy. It may seem strange to approach philosophy through a study of art, but I think that today there is good reason for doing just this. Philosophy, as the love of wisdom, is a concern for what is ultimate; and to express and develop such a concern requires a context in which technical detail, extraneous demands for precision, practical interests, and the need for a sophisticated grasp of an extremely complex situation can be set aside. There was a time, for example in ancient Greece, when philosophy could be approached through a consideration of the name and nature of knowledge. But this could be done then only because knowledge had not been identified with science, and a discussion of it could be carried on without inevitable involvement in specialized theory, the implications of practical control, and the presupposition of an arduous technical training. I do not doubt that philosophy may be approached today through a science, say, mathematics; but to do so means that one limits one's audience to a group of experts, who must be asked to set aside their expertise and consider their subject in a radically different way than their training and the pressures of society would suggest to them.

Philosophy may be approached through art in relation to a much broader audience, for a great many men today stand in relation to art as the Greeks stood in relation to knowledge. Perhaps, in principle, the only men today who do not stand in this relation are the artists themselves, who must, in virtue of their special commitment, take a more specialized view of their discipline. Thus, I suggest, art today provides an open way to philosophy, better now than the path through knowledge; and better too, because more open, than the path followed in the Middle Ages through religion.

I trust, then, that any reader who begins these pages with an interest in and a desire to think about and reflect upon art will find much to satisfy him in these terms. But I hope, too, that such a reader will be led to the threshold of philosophy and placed in a position where he must decide either to cross that threshold or to remain within the context of everyday life.

JOHN M. ANDERSON

University Park, Pennsylvania
August, 1967

ACKNOWLEDGMENTS

The author gratefully acknowledges the permission granted by the following publishers to quote from their publications:

Doubleday & Co. for a Haiku of Basho in *Zen Buddhism* by D. T. Suzuki, edited by William Barrett.

Harcourt Brace & World, Inc. for the "Mask of Evil" and excerpts from "A Grand Chorale of Thanksgiving" from *Selected Poems* by Bertolt Brecht, translated by H. R. Hays; and lines from *Murder in a Cathedral* by T. S. Eliot.

Oxford University Press for a manuscript version of Blake's "Tiger," from *The Poetical Works of William Blake*, edited by John Sampson.

Random House, Inc. for excerpts from *Strange Interlude* by Eugene O'Neill.

George Allen & Unwin, Ltd. and Alfred A. Knopf, Inc. for Po Chü-i's "Last Poem" from *Chinese Poems* by Arthur Waley.

The Committee of the Central Fund for Research of The Pennsylvania State University has provided funds which have aided materially in completing the manuscript.

My debt to other writers on art and the philosophy of art is far too extensive to be acknowledged in a brief statement. I wish, however, to record my obligations to Heinrich Zimmer, whose books on Indian art, religion, and civilization first introduced me to materials I have found most suggestive for the development of my own thought.

This book began in a course of lectures given at The Free University of Berlin in the Summer Semester of 1962. It developed during a number of seminars at The Pennsylvania State University. I appreciate the many discussions with my students, and their criticism, suggestions, and encouragement. I am indebted to Mr. Merritt Weidner for suggestions concerning examples, and to Dr. Barbara Panzl for considerable help with examples and with other problems of style and presentation.

CONTENTS

1 THE BEGINNINGS OF ART   3

    I   Ordinary Experience and Aesthetic Vision   3
   II   The Art-Object and Aesthetic Vision   10
  III   An Ephemeral Vision and Man   17

2 THE ART-WORK   25

    I   Art and Action   25
   II   Form and Content   33
  III   Process and the Aesthetic Occasion   38
  IV   Figure, Symmetry and Realm   42

3 REFLEXIVE FORMS   51

    I   Human Meaning and Value in Art:
        Expression   51
   II   Forming by Contrast and Function:
        Inception   56
  III   Forming by Exfoliation: Presence   63
  IV   Patterns of Creation: Art Forms and
        Renewal   78
   V   Man's Place in Art   89

4 TRANSCENDENTAL FORM: COMEDY   95

    I   Negative Elements   95
   II   The Comic and the Comic Form   106
  III   The Comedy of Appearance   120

5 TRANSCENDENTAL FORM: TRAGEDY   131

    I   Intuition of the Hero   131
   II   Man's Fate   138
  III   The Heroic Movement   151

6 HORIZONAL FORM: THE SUBLIME 163

 I Beauty 163
 II The Sublime 169
 III Man and Art 183

APPENDIX 185

INDEX 187

THE REALM OF ART

CHAPTER 1

THE BEGINNINGS OF ART

I. *Ordinary Experience and Aesthetic Vision*

When we approach art we have a choice to make. We may observe, first, that the history of man is also a history of art, for there has been no time in man's past when art was not a part of his life. The drawings in prehistoric caves are an instance of a human activity as common today as it was then. Contemporary ceramics are as invariably decorated and aesthetically shaped as were those of primitive peoples. So pervasive is art that to understand a culture of today or of the past we must approach it in part, at least, in the terms of its characteristic artistic activities. Where man is or has been, there art is to be found as well.

In this sense art is a fact, and what more is to be said about it is to be said in the terms of some other discipline than art. There is a history of art and a psychology of art, to mention two examples. Such disciplines deal descriptively with art in relation to other human activities and to the world. Yet there seems to be more to art than such disciplines capture. We may observe, secondly, that art arrests us, holds us, transfixes us. It pulls our attention away from other affairs, and we come to rest within it. Such characteristics of art seem opposed to its factual nature. They suggest that art is an ultimate beyond which one cannot go, and which, as such, cannot be dealt with in any other terms than its own. Let us choose to consider art in this sense.

Of all the areas with which one must deal in their own

terms, such as mathematics or religion, art is that one which results in the most confusion and distortion when taken in this way. This is attested by an odd reluctance on the part of many persons who are attracted to art to participate in art in its own terms. Children tend to live in the lands of tale and story as if these were an extension of their ordinary lives. There is nothing odd in this, since children enter the realm of art without noticing the threshold which they cross. Adults, by contrast, often respond to art in the terms of the ordinary world. It is not unusual for viewers of a TV serial, or listeners to a radio series, for example, to write to the characters in the drama (in care of the studio, of course), admonishing them of dangers they may encounter in the future episodes of the series, and advising them of desirable practical and moral behavior under the circumstances. Nor is it uncommon for members of an audience to remark of a play, "It's exactly like life." They don't mean this, for no play is exactly like life—it couldn't be. What they do mean is that they are responding to the play in the terms of their usual responses to life. When this occurs the ultimate significance of art is reduced to that of ordinary experience. Such a reaction is not a naïve failure to notice a threshold to be crossed; it reflects a kind of personal inability to cross the threshold in spite of the possibility and attraction of doing so.

We may note such inability, often unconsciously but elaborately developed, on the part of individuals whose personalities are characterized by their quest for explicitness, as in those having a strong propensity for intellectual analysis. Such intellectuals may react to art which attracts them by seeking to encompass it within the existing conceptual apparatus of their understanding. The ultimacy of art may be ignored by means of a historical study of the life of the artist. In place of entering into art, explicitly comprehensible peripheral materials—such as the dates of paintings or musical compositions, details about the development of the artist's techniques, or the psychology of the artist and its effect on his creative activity—become the focus of attention. Such intellectual response to art may encompass a historical period. An analysis of the period then becomes the central preoccupation, and readily formulable principles of different schools of art are elicited and the lines of mutual influences and development are traced out. Such analysis is the web of an intellectual personality spread over the door to art, effectively screening its ultimacy.

Other examples of intellectual response which precludes taking art in its own terms include those critics who express their attraction to art by formulating rules for judging it. Such rules as "The test of art is the touchstone of the masters" or "Good art communicates universal human emotion" no doubt have some aesthetic significance. Yet the very use of these rules in evaluating art emphasizes techniques of judging rather than art. The sort of analytical criticism which sets art in the context of psychoanalytic categories, or, say, Marxist philosophical concepts, or mathematical analysis (of the curves and surfaces of Greek pottery, for example) also evidently substitutes a mode of analysis for a concern with art.

Tolstoi traduces the categories congenial to intellectual criticism:

> Critics explain! What do they explain? The artist, if a real artist, has by his work transmitted to others the feeling he experienced. What is there, then, to explain?

The categories of the intellect are, however, not the only ones which stand between man and a response to art in its own terms. An emotional reaction to art may do this even more effectively, just because the feelings triggered by art are more apt to express the quality of our emotional character than to be appropriate to the nature of art. An emotional response is often a pathetic response: it expresses our affective nature as this has been developed in the context of ordinary living.

Even more obviously, a practical reaction to art avoids dealing with it as ultimate. Taking art as if it were merely a part of the world of practical affairs is not particularly unusual. On this basis the opera becomes a place to meet our associates and to be seen, we buy and display paintings to express social position (or to acquire it), and we understand novels and plays as throwing light on psychological problems or social issues.

Where strong intellectual, emotional, or practical personalities are found, the dominance of the response pattern determined by such a character may preclude dealing with art in its own terms. If possible, this is even truer where there is a strong propensity to take a moral view of life. Moral response to art is common. We condemn villains, praise the virtue of heros, condone or favor official censorship. If few would agree with Tolstoi that the true function of art is moral education, many do agree that art is a part of the world of morality, and is to be judged in moral terms. Such people remain moralists in the face of art, and respond to it only through the moral issues raised in and by it. We see here another instance of a certain ambivalence in human orientation toward art. On the one hand, man is attracted to art. But on the other hand, he may and often does structure his responses to it in ways which conceal its fundamental nature. This is not inevitably the case, however, and occasionally man comes to an encounter with art in its own terms, almost by accident, within the structures determined by his own nature.

One might suppose that what would be of interest in human history would be what reflects the overt and obvious patterns of man's present life. We might imagine the goal of historical enquiry to be the establishment of the nature of those human activities and institutions which mirror in the past the central preoccupations of our present life. This is one of the goals of historical research; but we find in the past a significance of a different sort as well; for example, the significance of its art. When we turn to the past to learn something about our present concerns, an accidental encounter with ancient art can focus our attention far more sharply than does our initial quest. We may seek to comprehend the nature of Greek democracy and to understand the structure of Greek society. But once we have come upon the splendor of Greek temples, the poetry of Homer, or the living quality of Greek sculpture, we are caught and held in this art. Similarly we may learn much of contemporary significance from the culture of the Middle Ages; but when we have

7

encountered medieval cathedrals with their carvings and stained glass, we are held in a developing experience of them.

When thrown back into the past the net of our present concerns catches the unexpected, for it catches art. Some of the art caught is impressive, so arresting that it changes the basis of our concern for the past. We study the Greek language in order better to encounter Greek poetry, epics, and drama. Having discovered Greek literature and the monuments and architecture of this people, we again turn to study their civilization in order to respond more fully to their art. If the art of a culture is good enough it motivates and sustains our interest in comprehending the life of the period, and this interest then serves to provide a path leading more deeply into that art.

It is sometimes claimed that this peculiar centrality of art in our dealings with the past is due to the fact that art expresses and communicates as does nothing else. The art of the past, it is said, expresses ordinary human meanings more clearly than do the political patterns, the technical accomplishments, or the moral codes of ancient times. This claim seems unwarranted. Indeed, the art of the past is obscure and strange as is nothing else. Ancient art is strange to us, for example, partly because we do not see it in the context of the overt patterns and explicit meanings which were a part of ancient culture and which tended to obscure art for ancient peoples, as such contemporary patterns and meanings obscure art for us. The temples of Greece do not have the religious meanings for us which they had for the ancient Greeks. The churches of the Middle Ages are not churches for us (even

8

when we are believers) in the same ways as they were for those peoples who built them and worshipped in them. In our dealings with the past, art may emerge as ultimate just because these dealings carry us out of the patterns which dominate our responses in contemporary life and may not replace them with similar ancient patterns. Even though we look to the past with the intention of discovering what life was like at that time, we may not find this out soon enough to prevent a half-accidental encounter with art. We may come upon art unexpectedly and in its own terms in the study of history.

The study of the past sometimes serves as a path to art. A museum, too, may serve as such a path. Usually, of course, museums are built for various explicit ends, such as the expression of national or local pride, for the housing of conquered art, as an acceptable public expression of private wealth, or to aid the study of cultural history. When we visit a museum we may do so to serve these ends or more personal goals of a similar sort. We may go to a museum to pass the time in a strange city, to learn something, to impress our friends. Yet whatever the explicit aim which carries us into a museum or which led to its construction, to enter it is to step to the limits of activities which ordinarily dominate our lives. To enter a museum is to step, momentarily, out of the context of ordinary behavior patterns, a step which leaves us temporarily in a condition to encounter art in its own terms. In consequence, when we enter a museum we may step into the realm of art.

The study of history and the visiting of museums are instances of ill-defined paths leading into the realm of art.

There are other such ill-defined paths, as, for example, the collection of art-objects or, even, discussion and criticism of art. These paths are ill defined because the signposts along them point to goals other than an encounter with art. But the fact that such paths may be misused, as it were, suggests the possibility that we may enter the realm of art; and the use of such paths for this unstated purpose is evidence that we desire to move into this realm. A less accidental and better path into the realm of art is to be found through the art-objects which an artist gives to us and which we preserve for just this purpose.

II. *The Art-Object and Aesthetic Vision*

Any art-object, when we come to examine it closely, appears to possess characteristics which constitute obstacles to our usual response patterns. When we try to deal with an art-object in the modes of our ordinary personality, to catch it in the explicit structures of practice, understanding, emotion, or morality, it eludes us. Relative to these responses it appears ambiguous and misleading. Yet there is often little doubt that the artist intended to make it this way, that the difficulties interposed in the way of plain and obvious response were deliberately introduced. We have only to think of lyric poetry, of abstract painting, of atonal music to have this sense of the artist's intention.

What is the significance of this intention? Why is it important that ordinary responses to an art-object be prevented; that an art-object should evoke from us a different kind of response than that which is typical of the quest for explicitness which structures our ordinary living? An important function of any art-object is to provide a path to art, and to make this path a better one than is available through ordinary experience. To function in this way the art-object must evoke different responses from us than our ordinary ones, for unless it does so the path it affords us cannot be better than an approach to art through history or criticism, for example. Aesthetic responses must be aroused and encouraged, and it is to this end that the art-object is so peculiarly structured, that its character is so markedly different from what we expect of objects in other areas of our living.

Many properties of art-objects call for responses which are out of the ordinary. For example, poetry characteristically focuses our attention upon sounds, and it holds our attention there. Consider the first lines of Nietzsche's poem "Vereinsamt":

> Die Krähen schreien
> Und Ziehen schwirren Flugs zur Stadt:
> Bald wird es schneien.
> Wohl dem, der jetzt noch eine Heimat hat!

Here the sounds are so insistent, their pattern so intricate, that they preoccupy us to the exclusion of, say, the kind of analytical understanding of the sentences which could relate them to our everyday interests and activities. Of course, this effect is not the result of emphasis on sound alone, for the imagery and ideas presented serve in the same way and do it well, since they are so striking. For these reasons, too, the opening lines of William Blake's

11

poem, "The Marriage of Heaven and Hell," are good examples of poetic sentences:

> Rintrah roars and shakes his fires in the burdened air;
> Hungry clouds swag on the deep.

And so are the lines of nursery rhymes, such as:

> Hyder iddle diddle dell,
> A yard of pudding's not an ell:
> Not forgetting tweedle-dye,
> A tailor's goose will never fly.

Here the sounds and images do not combine to form a consistent picture in ordinary human terms. Indeed, the writing of such lines seems to have introduced conflict and contradiction, even irrelevance, to prevent just this consistent comprehension of them. And in a poem of the Japanese poet Basho, which in English translation runs:

> A branch shorn of leaves
> A crow perching on it
> This autumn eve.

there is an evident use of mutually irrelevant images to prevent an ordinary response.

The use of rhyme and meter in poetry, or of cadence in prose, often contributes to the prevention of ordinary response. For example, rhyme and meter in poetry focus our attention upon ordinarily irrelevant sounds, words, and images; and in so doing they distract our attention from those parts of a poem which could be selected and put together to form a clear picture reflecting man's practical, emotional, or moral concerns. So long as the rhymed words hold us, so long as the meter evokes a response, so long as alliteration fascinates, we cannot grasp the poem within the patterns so useful to us, patterns which reflect that human nature which dominates our ordinary experience. If we respond to the poem it must be in a different way; and because of this the artist cuts a path along which we may move into art. When Gerard Manley Hopkins begins his poem "Nature is a Heraclitean Fire":

> Cloud-puffball, torn tufts, tossed pillows flaunt forth, then chevy on an air-
> built thoroughfare; heaven-roysterers, in gay-gangs they throng; they glitter in marches.
> Down roughcast, down dazzling whitewash, wherever an elm arches,
> Shivelights and shadowtackle in long lashes lace, lance, and pair.

he tries to prevent us from moving within the obvious reaches of our experience, forcing us to break these bounds. To the extent that he succeeds there is a path, at least, to art.

We find the same kinds of characteristics serving similar purposes in art-objects other than poems. In painting, for example, lines and the patterns of lines and their symmetries, as well as colors and color arrangements catch and hold our attention. In Van Gogh's work arbitrary forms and bursts of color focus our attention upon aspects of the painting which can hardly be incorporated into practical seeing or easy comprehension. The flesh tones and composition of curves and planes in the paintings of Botticelli have the same effect of serving as obstacles to certain kinds of responses to the art-object. In music, the use of pitch, value, and timbre in the composition of tones, the use of scales as organizing patterns, the presence of rhythms, and the patterns of harmony all fix our awareness in such a way that we participate in *music* rather than the noises which we ordinarily hear put together in human language, or the noises which we hear as audible signs of practical importance in the world of everyday experience.

Evidently there is a variety of artistic techniques and a resulting variety of characteristics of the art-object which serve to make it difficult to respond to this object as we habitually respond to most objects. One function of these characteristics is negative: they are introduced, in part at least, to prevent obvious responses. Thus neither a catalog of them, nor a systematic analysis of their nature is important. For one thing, the ways of achieving a negative result are so many and depend to so great an extent upon the accidents of time and circumstance as to defy classification. For another, many of the devices used to prevent an easy response to the art-object have no direct connection with the happening of art; they are not constitutive of art, and we need observe only that they exist. Thus, for example, any characteristic of an art-object which shocks can serve this negative function: as strange colors, obscenity, senselessness. But what will shock is so relative to culture and conditioning as to make an account of it of no general importance.

The pertinent general observation is that man's responses to circumstances tend to become expressions of his struggle toward comprehension, so that his ordinary responses to things are dominated by his quest toward explicit form, toward full expression. Certainly many of the devices used in art-objects to prevent ordinary responses function by making it extraordinarily difficult for man to formulate the significance of these objects in any *one* way. By this means these devices break the tendency to respond in the terms of explicit forms. They break the limited patterns of responses focused on such forms.

Destruction of easy and definite response to the art-object is often achieved by the deliberate introduction of sources of ambiguity relative to the expected response. As already noted, emphasis on sound, stress, and rhythm in poetic discourse calls attention to words and phrases, and to ideas, in ways which prevent their forming a pattern reflecting man's quest for clear significance. The plot in a play may also function in this way, although it serves other artistic ends as well. In many cases these other functions of a plot may dominate, but occasionally the most important function of plot is simply the destruction of ordinary human response to the art-object. This is the case, for example, in the series of plays which have been written around the legend of the birth of Hercules. There are various versions of the myth itself dating from ancient times. There is also a play by Molière, another by Von Kleist, and one relatively recent drama by Giraudoux entitled *Amphitryon 38*, implying that this is the 38th version of the story.

Let us note the essentials of the myth. Hercules is an important figure in Greek mythology: his birth is significant. In the myth, Hercules' father was Zeus and his mother was Amphitryon's wife, Alcmene. At some point in the retelling of this myth, an artist noted that Amphitryon was a courageous and respected man who had served his country well, and that his wife was a devoted and virtuous woman. Thus the seduction of Alcmene by Zeus presents problems, for although the moral behavior of Zeus is far from exemplary, he *is* a god of justice and must be expected to behave justly. Amphitryon's wife is virtuous, yet she is seduced. Zeus is a god, yet he must cuckold a patriotic and honorable man, and seduce a virtuous woman.

To some extent we can accept Alcmene's seduction if Zeus achieves his goal through the impersonation of Amphitryon, and this device has been widely used in retelling the myth. However, such an impersonation raises other problems; for then Zeus, although having the power of a god, is forced to impersonate Amphitryon and act as a man in order to gain his end. If we try to say clearly what does happen in the play, so developed, it is not easy. When the situation leading to the birth of Hercules is depicted in this way, it seems to defy comprehension within the patterns expressing obvious emotional, moral, practical, or intellectual principles. Was Alcmene seduced? We know that Hercules was born, for this is the evidence of history. Zeus seems to have achieved this end by becoming Amphitryon, so that Alcmene seems only to have slept with her husband. Was Zeus a god? We know that he was reduced to impersonating Amphitryon to carry out the patterns of history, yet surely the power of a god is required for such an impersonation. Was Amphitryon mistreated? Apparently Zeus cuckolds him, yet it was as Amphitryon that Zeus slept with Alcmene. Intellectually the picture makes no sense, and morally it makes no sense—it makes no sense except the sense of comedy. But to experience comedy is to have been led beyond our ordinary responses, and into art. The construction of the plot has served the purpose of preventing ordinary responses; and, at least, has built a path along which we may be led into comedy and so, into art.

When viewed exclusively as fulfilling a negative function, art-objects may appear as having a negative character; that is, as ambiguous, polyvalent, senseless, irrelevant. If the artist, by any of the means suggested, prevents our ordinary responses to the art-object, he does not reduce us to the kind of idiocy, intellectual confusion, moral nihilism, or neurotic frustration which the use of these means might suggest. If he does not reduce us to such a state, it must be because he offers us, through the art-object, the basis for another kind of response, a response different from, but a substitute for, the kind of response he prevents. In a play about Amphitryon we actually do come to move in the world of comedy—emerging into this world, among the shattered fragments of moral codes, disrupted prudential behavior, and intellectual patterns. When the authors of these plays prevent our ordinary responses, they open for us, sometimes at least, an alternative world. It is this world which is the realm of art, and which we must consider next in its relation to man's personality and his nature.

III. An Ephemeral Vision and Man

In our human perspective, that is, the perspective which is opened through our ordinary intellectual, moral, practical, and emotional responses, we come upon the aesthetic

17

vision by accident, and its strangeness overwhelms us. We set the experience, built through such responses, aside in favor of a chance development of another kind of experience. Even when the artist aids, as it were, this chance encounter by making an art-object which helps to set aside our human perspective, the emphasis is still upon negating, upon destroying, obvious patterns of response and the experience they build. Artists often seem well aware of this. Thus Yeats tells us, "All art is *reaction from life* . . ." and Blake, equating life and memory, hopes "To cast off the rotten rags of memory by inspiration . . ."

The point is put more strongly when Blake says, "I come in self-annihilation and the grandeur of inspiration . . ." Here he implies that destroying the ordinary patterns of human response involves a destruction of the ego, the personality of the artist, as well. Keats refers to the same consequence when he observes, "A poet is the most unpoetical of anything in existence, because he has no Identity—he is continually in, for and filling some other body." Evidently, there is some truth in Rimbaud's blunt assertion, "Je *est* un autre," and in his methods of becoming this other by poisoning his own personality, by cultivating suffering, by torturing and distorting his senses.

But whichever way we like to put this point, whether as the destruction of those responses which lead into ordinary experience, or as a kind of freeing from the all-too-human personality which is the locus of such responses, there is a significant conclusion to be drawn. The success of this negative enterprise implies that there are aesthetic responses different from ordinary responses, and that there is a self emergent in aesthetic responses different from the ordinary personality. And it implies that these extraordinary responses develop into equally extraordinary awareness. Artists, and other lovers of art, have always insisted upon this conclusion. They use such phrases as "the realm of the imagination," "eternity," "waking dream" to suggest the different and exceptional quality of the aesthetic vision. Thus Blake tells us that "This world of Imagination is the world of Eternity . . ." But if such terms state the conclusion, they are not of sufficient help in understanding the exact nature of this extraordinary awareness. The reason for this lack is just the complexity of the relation of the "vision" to the "self" evoked by it. The understanding of this relation, indeed, is a basic task of the enquiry carried out in this book.

What Keats suggests when he says "O for a life of sensations rather than of thoughts!" is true; that is, in and through the senses we may escape from ordinary into aesthetic responses. To live such a life we sometimes have only to strike a key on the piano and let the tone carry us, or to draw a line of a pure color on a tablet and let it hold our attention. How much more, then, can the artist offer us such a life in the rich sounds of complex music or in the rich colors of painting! The materials of the senses, of smell, of taste and touch, of hearing and sight, are among those to which the artist turns to make possible his and our aesthetic response. Yet these materials, these sensations, are not passive content of his and our awareness, they are not simply *presented*. Rather, they are part of a situation involving intense activity.

Listen to Gerard Manley Hopkins who begins by noticing some bluebells, and is caught up in something more, and more confusing, than this sight:

> This day and May 11 the bluebells in the little wood . . . stood in blackish spreads . . . It was a lovely sight.—The bluebells in your hand baffle you with their inscape, made to every sense: if you draw your fingers through them they are lodged and struggle with a shock of wet heads; the long stalks rub and click and flatten to a fan on one another like your fingers themselves would when you passed the palms hard across one another, making a brittle rub and jostle like the noise of a hurdle strained by leaning against; then there is the faint honey smell and in the mouth the sweet gum when you bite them. But this is easy, it is the eye they baffle. They give one a fancy of pan-pipes and of some wind instrument with stops—a trombone perhaps. The overhung necks—for growing they are little more than a staff with a simple crook but in water, where they stiffen, they take stronger turns, in the head like sheephooks or, when more waved throughout, like waves riding through a whip that is being smacked—what with those overhung necks and what with the crisped ruffled bells dropping mostly on one side and the gloss these have at their footstalks they have an air of the knights of chess . . .

What began with the immediacy but also with the sense of distance and passivity of sight changes: first, into the activity of participation more typical of touch, smell, and taste; finally, into the *active* vision which replaces the beginning, the rather ordinary "lovely sight," with a developing polyvalence of unexpected patterns and confusion of meanings.

The human aspect of active participation in such a circumstance is often referred to as intuitive experience, and the developing content of this participation as intuition. It may seem that to replace a phrase like "waking dream" with "intuitive experience," and to substitute for "realm of the Imagination" the word "intuition," is to gain very little in clarity and understanding. Perhaps not, but it may be possible to develop a complex use of the word intuit, and to come to see something of what it ought to connote. To this end we may note in Hopkins' account that intuitive experience develops from response to the given immediacy of sense materials, and, more important, that the active response which develops it gives it the special character of opening to unexpected content, that is, of adumbrating intuitions.

Whitman's "Song of Myself" illustrates these important points further. There Whitman has a good deal to say about the place of the senses and aesthetic response: "I think I will do nothing now but listen . . . to let sounds contribute toward me . . . Is this then a touch? quivering me to a new identity." Whitman declares emphatically that the immediacy of sense is not passive reception: "Flames and ether making a rush for my veins/ Treacherous tip of me reaching and crowding to help them . . ." That the unexpected content evokes a new identity for man is explicit in Whitman's phrasing; and it is also obvious that in this evocation there is a loss of the ordinary self of which Whitman speaks when he says "I am given up by traitors; I talk wildly—I have lost my wits—I and nobody else am the greatest traitor . . ."

It is not only the senses which are traitors to the ordinary self. In music, a composer often falls back upon folk melodies and folk themes and upon primitive rhythms in the hopes that these may call forth his (and our) aesthetic response. The painter, too, often depicts the Madonna, or an idyllic landscape, or a hunting scene for similar reasons. Or he may use old designs and symmetries with the expectation that these can evoke an aesthetic response. We may see something of the peculiar significance of myth in art in such usage. The situations, protagonists, and plots which are the forms of myth, and in a way its substance as well, often seem to call us to extraordinary responses. Stories of exile, of the emergence of individuality, of destroying love, of the hatred of brothers, of man's relation to the gods have this effect in part because of their immediacy. In this, like folk melodies and old designs, they involve us more directly than do other materials and betray us surprisingly often, so that we are carried out of our ordinary selves into intuitive experience and toward intuition.

At one time in our lives, no doubt, we were involved in learning to hear, to see, to taste, to touch, and to smell; that is, we learned to sense. But this happened long ago, so long ago that we have forgotten the process, if we ever were aware of it. So far as the materials of sense go we do not distinguish ordinarily between what is given to our senses and what we make of this. In developing an aesthetic situation the artist makes possible just this distinction; that is, when successful he is able to revive an awareness of the process which begins with the opacity of the given and carries over into its differentiation and articulation. In this awareness there is a reference to what is merely given and to its articulation. What essentially characterizes such process and such awareness as aesthetic is that the given and its articulation are held together there

in the unfinished movement of becoming. It is the awareness of the union afforded by this movement which we
call intuitive experience, and it is the eventuation of this
movement in forms grasped as continuously grounded in
the given which we call intuition.

The use in music of folk melodies and primordial
rhythms, the depiction in painting of age-old designs and
themes, and the wide use of myth throughout most art
forms may be understood in the same terms as those just
formulated in respect to the use of sense materials. Here,
too, the weld between what is given and the forms which
articulate it was made so long ago in man's history as to
seem to us, from our ordinary perspective, to be no joint
at all. Yet here, too, the artist may be able to revive an
awareness of the joining process and the relation of what
is joined by the careful use of artistic devices. The deliberate introduction of unusual stress, order, and sound into
the words, lines, and symmetries, or into the tones and
musical phrases of an art-object, makes ordinary responses
difficult if not impossible. What is then made possible is
an awareness of sense materials, folk melodies or myth,
for example, in which the darkness of the given comes to
be lighted through an articulating movement. But there
is an awareness, too, in which such articulation supports
the artist's and our sense of the bond between the merely
given and its forms, that awareness of disclosed content
we call intuition.

The painter, Kandinski, puts the point this way: "I
painted . . . pictures in which I wished to bury in each
part an 'infinite' number of initially hidden color tones.
They had to remain completely *hidden* at first (especially
in the dark part) and only as time went on show them-

selves, at first unclearly and tentatively, to the studiously attentive viewer, then resound more and more with an increasingly '*mysterious*' power."

The loss of personality, the destruction of the ordinary ego, which is an aspect of aesthetic response, is related to this new awareness, for this awareness, in part, is comprised of the sense of unity which reflects the bond between the merely given and the patterns which come to form it. It is this sense of unity which replaces the sense of personal identity based upon the structure of ordinary responses, as we are carried in artistic activity into the process uniting the given and its patterns. Yet the self which is evoked through man's participation in art is much more than this, and more extraordinary. It is not merely the reflection of the process welding together the given and its articulation, for this occurs in a limited and transient way, whereas the sense of this unity which is evoked in man projects beyond such occurrences, and, indeed, functions as a standard for the process in question. The mysterious power which we feel the emergence of articulated patterns to have, is to be understood when we see it as supporting the claim made by the self evoked by art— that the articulation of the merely given ought to be supported and continued. The extraordinary self evoked by man's participation in art expresses such a claim and is involved in its support. It is this which introduces much of the complexity into the artist's and the appreciator's relation to art. To understand this we must turn, first, to a study of the process of which aesthetic response is a part.

CHAPTER 2

THE ART WORK

I. Art and Action

The advent of action painting in the twentieth century provides an instance of artists who emphasize the activity of creation, who simply *paint*. Thus there is a sense in which de Kooning or Hans Hoffman, for example, can be said to enact a painting, to enter upon the canvas and participate in something there, to produce lines consisting of strokes and figures which extend the actual motion of the artist's body. Such lines and figures release force upon the canvas and testify to a forming which makes the art an event. As an event the painting has a beginning; it has a duration, direction can be discerned in it, there is passivity and concentration, relaxation and intensity, waiting and fulfillment within it; and quite possibly it has an ending. These moments of action, to be found in abstract expressionism, are moments of forming in which the artist participates, and they demand a repetition of this participation from the appreciator. The appreciator, with the help provided by the artist, reenters the painting, reconstructs it; and his aesthetic experience is a quality of his activity. But what is this art?

Certainly one of the reactions of the critics and of the public generally has been a confessed failure to find in action painting the usual values of art. Curators display this work without presuming to decide whether it is art or not; they even point out in the catalogs of their exhibits that action painting lacks standards and criteria for judgment, that there is really no way of telling which is the better painting and which is the worse. Such curators, and members of the public, too, often attribute their posture of despair in this regard to the lack of "form" in expressionistic painting. How, they ask rhetorically, can we judge or evaluate art in which there is action but no explicit form?

The impact of art on man and his consequent concern with it are too great to permit the question of aesthetic judgment to remain rhetorical. Contact with art, participation in it, seems to demand of man a discernment of its principle and an evaluation of its ultimacy. Thus, if the question of aesthetic judgment is not answered in the terms of art itself, it comes to be answered in terms external to art. For example, it may be that over the course of future years critics will develop a new set of criteria relevant to action painting, and will then claim an ability to judge this art. But such a claim transfers the task of producing art from the artist to the critic, a result more paradoxical for aesthetic judgment than the advent of action painting. Such a transfer has taken place in the past; and, indeed, is now taking place. When it occurs it changes the function of the critic and art historian from that of recognizing art in its own terms to that of determining what art is. This is a function which comes to be exercised by making a place for art-objects in art history, and then by assuming, usually tacitly, that art comprises nothing but such objects in art history. In the end this reduces art to its history, and in so doing it divorces the standards of art from art itself.

The problem of this mistaken reduction—so prevalent today—is deeper than this contemporary statement of it might suggest, for all art has something of the character attributed to action painting. For an older but evident instance consider Sumiye painting. The art of Sumiye painting is an ancient one in Japan. It is pursued in a way which, initially, seems designed to prevent the achievement of any significant result. But, as a matter of fact, it is this paradoxical method which gives exactly the results which are desired. The Sumiye painter makes his picture by drawing with an inked brush on paper. Of course this is not unusual. However, the ink used is composed of soot and glue and the brush is often made of sheep's wool. In addition the paper used is thin and absorbent. In consequence it is necessary to paint very quickly; otherwise the paper will absorb too much ink and be torn as the brush moves across it. No deliberation is possible; no erasing; no repetition; no retouching. So the result of such painting is an accident achieved by spontaneous and free drawing. There is no deliberate representation, for the nature of the method and the conditions of its practice prevent the drawing *of* something; and they prevent the introduction of perspective or coloring. In such an act of painting, the forms produced do not stand between the artist and a scene. In the act of painting in this tradition the content of the painting emerges; in the act of forming the artist elicits content, as a dot becomes a man or a bird, a line becomes a mountain, and the artist's actions become a part of the painting which he helps to build.

But we need not refer only to such esoteric painting. The representative painting of many recent water-colorists might be described in much the same way. John Marin, for example, painted a great many scenes with considerable speed, producing a number of sheets of water colors; he then preserved only those which happened to turn out well. It is common practice in water color technique today to proceed with great speed and freedom, to use wet colors, to hold the paper at different angles to allow the paint to run in various ways; and to destroy all but a few of the results. When water color painting is pursued in this way there is an emphasis upon the evocation of formed materials, the emergence of content; there is entry into a painting, partly through the activities of the artist and partly through accident. For in these cases the result is not a deliberate intention of the artist; he destroys those sheets which do not turn out well, preserving only those which *in his judgment* have led into art.

The issue is whether the artist is entitled to exercise his judgment in determining art; whether the artist comes to stand in a special place with respect to art, or whether the true nature of art is to be discerned after the fact and on a different basis than the terms of the artist's participation in art. Underlying this issue, and contributing greatly to the difficulty of resolving it, is the apparently transient, even ephemeral character of man's contact with art. For all our concern with art, for all our sense of its ultimacy, it comes to us in ways which seem touched with illusion, it appears caught up in the moment, sensuous and evanescent, new and passing. Certainly this has been implicit in our discussion in Chapter One of the relations of art to ordinary experience. And it is a point which has often been noted. There is not much doubt that Poe has this in mind when he explains that "All excitements are through a psychal necessity, transient," and adds that half an hour is the utmost time during which "that degree of excitement which would entitle a poem to be so called at all" could endure.

So emphatic is this sense of transience that artists have often seen it as of the essence, and have formulated their conception of art with this in mind. Certainly Poe wishes to suggest this in the passage quoted. And Paul Klee, in his *Creative Credo* argues that time is required for a dot to turn into a line, for a line to form a surface, and for the picture to develop: quite evidently he is insisting that movement and action are the essence of art. Yet once such a concession is made, is it really possible to find the true nature of art in the midst of this change and transience? Will it not be necessary to find stability and universality beyond art, in the intellectual patterns of history, for example? How else could one interpret the use of newspapers in collage to date art (as practiced by Picasso)? Or how else view the example of Tinguely in producing self-annihilating sculpture which literally stands for awhile in history and then vanishes? Isn't this the significance of the French painter Mathieu's credo when he performs the act of painting in public, making of it a spectacle, as if the reality of art were to be found in its performance, its occurrence in time? And what possible alternative is open when we observe the abolition of the distinction between artist and appreciator in those cases where the audience attending museums and galleries is asked to add to the art displayed there, contributing colors and objects and forms to what has been called Merzbau?

Evidently the aesthetic credos of these modern artists constitute one version of the sense in which transience and change are close to the center of art. They offer a literal account of this insight; and they provide, when put into practice in the ways mentioned, a good deal of support for the claim that there are no standards of judgment to be found in art itself, for these practices reduce art to literal events in the stream of time. These practices suggest that a sound response to art can be made only by determining periods in an artist's life, tracing out developing lines of influence, defining schools, and in other ways providing historical handles. Where the practice seemingly implied by these aesthetic credos leaves us baffled by their reduction of art to events, such historical handles give a semblance of understanding. Yet it is an understanding which finds in art nothing but a place in the sequence of time.

Neither Poe nor Klee would have been satisfied with these consequences of their claim that action is of the essence of art. It is clear that they made the statements quoted in order to call attention to art in its own terms. It is in order to insist that art is ultimate, that *art is its own sign,* that Poe and Klee call attention to the place of action in it. They emphasize the place of action in terms of the role of artist (and appreciator) as participating, believing that man as participant goes beyond the ephemeral, the merely human in art, to its true center. What leads to a misunderstanding of this point is not the stress on the activity of the artist; rather it is the interpretation of this activity as having its final result in the art-object, which then is seen as nothing more than a thing in history. To avoid this misunderstanding it is necessary to grasp the artist's activity as participation in disclosure of content, something which happens in an *art-work*, of which the art-object is but a by-product. The significance of disclosure of content, intuitively apprehended, is not its place in history, nor its mere occurrence in time in any sense. Its significance is to be found in itself. What is central for the artist, and for anyone who would judge art, is just this occasion.

The disclosure of content involves action as a necessary part of art, and it is the sense of this necessity which focuses and holds the attention of the artist. The understanding of the place and importance of action in art without a reduction of art to literal history is not as difficult as is implied by the dicta of contemporary critics and art historians, not to mention some artists. There is a long tradition of analysis of art in which form is understood as involving change and action. This tradition is found in the west as early as Aristotle, and it was continued by many, including Hegel and Bergson. However, if form is to be understood as involving the activity of forming, it is essential to make a sharp distinction between the art-object and something much more central to art which we have called the art-work. The activity of forming in painting has an art-object as a by-product, that is, the literal painted canvas, which might be used for aesthetically irrelevant purposes, such as patching a sail. Of more central importance, however, is the complex involving the artist, his creative actions, the literal and figurative materials used, the subject matter, the aesthetic experience, and other elements. It is of the essence that the activities of this complex lead into disclosure of content; and it is this dynamic complex which comprises the *art-work*.

That an art-work may come into being is attested in the dynamic complexes already mentioned—action painting, Sumiye painting, water-color painting. In each such case the aesthetic experience of the artist or appreciator involves disclosure of content; and in each case the complex comprises a kind of world of its own, a world in which the artist (and appreciator) may come to live and move, and have his aesthetic being. But let us consider another example. Whereas much of music is written down and then reproduced from such a record, this is rarely the case with jazz. Jazz is played often by musicians who know the themes and, in a sense, the pieces which they wish to play; but who work together to create an art-work through their cooperative efforts. The participants in jazz gather together to see what can be evoked. The world of music in which they move develops at the time of their active cooperation. This world is the art-work. Of course there is also an art-object—the literal music which might be recorded and then reproduced. And such an art-object makes possible a reconstruction of the world of jazz, a new art-work; but only for appreciators. The difference between the art-work and the art-object may be sharply stated by observing that the original artists cannot enter, as artists, into an art-work based on such reconstruction. And, in these terms, the difference between an artist and an appreciator is the relative independence of the by-product resulting from their artistic efforts. In the case of the artist the by-product is the art-object and comes to have a literal existence of its own; in the case of the appreciator the by-product ends in the configurations of imagination.

32

II. Form and Content

Form and content in an art-work are related in activity in complex ways. As the painter Robert Henri said:

> The object of painting a picture is not to make a picture . . . The picture . . . is a by-product and may be useful, valuable, interesting as a sign of what has passed. The object . . . is *the attainment of a state of being,* a state of high functioning, a more than ordinary moment of existence. In such moments activity is inevitable, and whether this activity is with brush, pen, chisel, or tongue, its result is but a by-product of the state, a trace, the footprint of the state.

If we try to be more specific about the locus of this state of high functioning, we may conceive of this in the case of a painting, certainly, as space. Yet if we do so locate it, there are a number of distinctions which need to be made. The first is that this space is not the literal spatial config-uration of the by-product, the painting. It is not the space which we apprehend as containing and forming the can-vas, the unevenness of the paint and brush strokes, the frame of the painting. This latter space is the space of the by-products of artistic activity, which as Henri also said:

> . . . become dear to the artist who made them because they are records of states of being which he has enjoyed and which he would regain. They are likewise interesting to oth-ers because they are to some extent readable and reveal the possibilities of greater existence.

But, second, the locus of our aesthetic participation is not in the space represented by the art-object, if, say, it is a landscape or a portrait. However, representation in painting may of course function to lead into the "space" of the art-work. This latter "space" is the one in which aesthetic participation takes place, and we may distinguish readily its variation in art-works which produce such different by-products as cubist paintings, the late line drawings of Picasso, Rembrandt's etchings, or Chinese paintings. This "space," better called a spatial complex to emphasize the distinctions just made, has special characteristics. Thus the complex generated in part through appreciative response to a Rembrandt etching is the matrix in which living objects emerge and relate to one another. Or the spatial complex of a classical Chinese landscape includes the appreciator quite explicitly, something which is suggested by the absence of any specific perspective in the space represented there.

One must make similar distinctions in speaking of time with reference to music or a novel. First, of course, there is the time it takes for a piece to be performed, or a novel to be read; this is clock time and measures the occurrence of the art-object. And, second, there is the time represented in a novel, the spread of events and circumstances which are depicted. In music the analogue of this represented time is called the time of the piece, that is, $\frac{2}{4}$ time, a movement performed *andante,* and so on; it is the underlying but changing beat of the music. No doubt represented time leads into the "time" of the art-work, which is better called a temporal complex. When we distinguish the movement in Sibelius' *Night Ride and Sun Rise* from that of Haydn's *Surprise Symphony,* say, we refer to this complex, for we speak of the complex of movement in which the

34

artist initially and we, as appreciators, subsequently are involved.

Such characteristics of this involvement in a dynamic complex mark it off sharply from experience developed in our ordinary responses. In ordinary experience, patterns, as literal space and time, tend to hide the materials which they form, whereas the aesthetic vision reveals content. But why does this difference arise? And what is its significance?

Ordinarily we apprehend content as veiled by forms, for ordinarily we are concerned primarily with the results *we* seek in our responses to circumstances. These results are the referential and designating import which form has for us. Ordinary experience focuses upon this aspect of form. More specifically, for example, our need to use a table focuses our attention upon its obvious spatial form as we seek, perhaps vainly, for an insight into the table's utility. Or, again, our need to reason with geometrical clarity brings to our attention the somewhat inadequate "squares" and "triangles" of the world of fact. Our struggle toward meaning and clarity highlights the forms of things; and, because these forms so grasped are more or less inadequate to our struggle, we see them as literal, as merely given, and as static. Thus our need for finding definite moral significance and insight *types* the men and women of our world; we are aware of them as moral characters and as determined by their character. Wherever our experience is dominated by our need for significance and clarity, wherever, for example, we seek practical, emotional, intellectual or moral meaning, there form holds our attention as a harbinger.

Yet this dominance of form is overcome wherever our experience is developed through our aesthetic responses. We may see this, in the crudest sense, by contrasting our practical awareness of direction markers, turn signals on automobiles, and advertisements, with our awareness of these signs as represented in paintings. In the world of ordinary experience their forms stand out; that is, we are aware of their forms as signifying, as having meanings. In the world of aesthetic experience their forms remain implicit; that is, we are aware of them as serving to reveal content. At a more complex level, we see that the interrelations introduced by the artist's palette into a painting serve to occasion the emergence of color. The use of complicated chords in music has the effect of revealing the constituent tones to us, for they emerge in this intrinsic pattern in a way which does not happen in the case of the elements of the noise of ordinary experience. And the use of intricate rhyming and stress patterns in poetry effectively presents words to us so that they appear with an intensity and splendor they never have in the context of practical communication.

This emerging of content in form, this revealing of immediate content, gives such an *aesthetic occasion* an ultimate, an absolute character which is found elsewhere but rarely. Some of the artist's activities are directed toward calling attention to this. That is, these activities function to direct the artist's attention—and, subsequently, our attention—away from ordinary experience; to take himself and us out of the world in which we ordinarily live; and to place himself and us in the midst of that emerging content which is central to the art-work. This task is accomplished in a variety of specific ways, but notably in poetry: for example, by rhyming, by the introduction of rhythm and stress patterns, by the expansion of attention, by alliteration, and the use of image and ambiguity. That is, the poet builds a situation in which signification and meaning are not seen as separated from the activities which underlie and support them. In poetry signification and meaning are set in the larger context of activity of which they and their occurrence are a part. The poet, and more generally the artist, intends to make possible an escape from an awareness limited to explicit forms to an awareness which includes the integral relation of form to content. Evidently the artist succeeds often enough in opening such an aesthetic occasion to himself and to us. Art has its beginnings in such success.

The connection between artistic activity and the ultimacy of art is not an accident or a miracle, although we may be ignorant of its nature. In artistic activity forms become a path developing an art-work, and so leading to an aesthetic occasion, that is, to an intuition. This is because in artistic activity forms are dealt with as *forming* and so as penetrating and eliciting content in such a way that it is encountered as one with these forms. When forms are handled in this way they permit movement along the path of the art-work where content emerges within the activity of forming, to be essentially articulated by form, to be a given part of an ultimate activity made up of form and content.

A function of aesthetic forming is the function of a path; a path which normally begins in relatively ordinary patterns, such as space and time, and develops toward the

37

emergence of content. Thus the artistic development of, say, space and time, the ways in which these forms are handled in art, evokes content. The forms with which artistic response begins are transmuted into forms which enfold content, as for example, do aesthetic space and time. This transmutation leads to an intuition, to an aesthetic occasion. Thus an aesthetic occasion is itself movement, something we need now to understand more fully.

III. Process and the Aesthetic Occasion

The materials of art disturb us, they are unquiet, uncanny. They serve to quicken us to move where we would otherwise not go—out of ourselves to become a part of we know not what. Such movement places us in the midst of an alien ongoing, as a part of a rush and movement which is foreign to us, in the midst of a process which lies partly beyond us. The attainment of this state is startling, but we may fail to grasp its significance. That is, we may suppose that *the* function of art is to carry us across a threshold. Art does have a ferrying function. Indeed, this function has been a subject of our discussion up to this point. Yet art has other functions as well. One of its major tasks is that of rendering significant the process into which it carries us, of revealing this as intuition.

Let us consider the art of painting. When one contrasts the colors which emerge in an art-work based upon a painting with the colors of ordinary experience, the especial character of the color in the art-work is evident enough. These colors have a vividness, an intensity, are luminously present in a way which distinguishes them from the rather drab occurrence of color in ordinary experience. Take note, for instance, of the startling color achieved by Van Gogh through the use of blue and yellow lines which are fused in the art-work into an amazing green. This is a new green, a revelation of what green can be. The colors which are disclosed in an art-work based upon a painting emerge through the forming in which the artist (and then the appreciator) participates in their emergence. The artist enters colors through his palette, and his palette is based upon his "theory" of color. Thus the pigments of a painting are evoked in relation to one another by the artist, and color emerges in the art-work.

In a similar way the introduction of complex chords in music relates sounds, revealing constituent tones in the art-work; something which does not happen in ordinary experience, for the noises there lack the requisite forming relations. Patterning by rhythm and rhyme in poetry interrelates words and their sounds to give an effect of uncommon intensity. A poem, that is, the art-work, martials words and parades them for our review to the accompaniment of their sounds. Thus they come out to us with a brilliant impact, appearing as they never do in normal context and use. And, for another instance, the movement of plot in a novel interrelates background, circumstance, and motivation in such a way as to disclose the protagonists as individuals. This is something which happens in everyday life only so far as we play the part of the novelist and plot the actions of the people we know.

These examples constitute prima facie evidence that forming activity involving an artist or appreciator in an art-work leads to the disclosure of content, to an aesthetic occasion. It is well known that vision is kinaesthetic, that what we see is seen in and through action. In order to perceive a line the eye must follow it, and the eye does this by a succession of acts of focusing, not by simply opening and serving as a lens through which light passes. These acts of focusing require muscular effort and control. The artist is tacitly aware of this, and when he draws a line in a picture he anticipates the mode of the appreciator's necessary kinaesthetic response. No doubt this is why Klee, for example, describes lines he has drawn and planes which they define in active terms: "An *active* line on a walk, moving freely, without a goal. A walk for a walk's sake. The mobility agent is a point, shifting its position forward." Or again; "Two secondary lines moving around an imaginary main line." And, of planes: "Passive angular lines and passive circular lines become active as planar constituents." Yet if kinaesthesis is the justification for Klee's statements and the explanation for our sense of action in drawn lines, it does not account for the fact that involvement in the drawing of such lines or in aesthetic response to them as drawn develops an art-work in which content emerges as formed. After all, kinaesthesis is involved in any perception, aesthetic or not.

Certainly when the artist draws a line in a picture he anticipates that the appreciator's kinaesthetic response will carry into the emerging content within the art-work, just as do his own activities. He thus expects kinaesthetic response in this case to terminate in intuition, to come to be forming which discloses content. When this happens, it is in consequence of the simple and completable activity of drawing of the artist, or of the simple and completable apprehension of the appreciator. To focus upon the example at hand; such activity discloses the points of a line, it makes of the line the form which reveals its parts, its points. The American artist, George Grosz, seems to have something of this sort in mind when he says:

> There must have been a reason for the invention of line. Yes, it is a guide for those who would venture into the formlessness that surrounds us on every side; a guide that leads us to the recognition of form and dimension and inner meaning . . . Line guides us when we would enter the Labyrinth of the countless millions of natural objects that surround us. Without line we would be soon lost; never would we be able to find our way again out of the maze.

We find our way out of the maze of perceived objects by movement along a line which forms given content and leads to a recognition of inner meaning. This movement is participation in the process which is the heart of the art-work, and which, essentially, comes to focus in an illumination of content, something we see as intuition. Thus this movement participates in the union of form and content and crystallizes in this unity.

Such disclosure of content would not occur if this kind of activity were not present. We may see this clearly if we compare sound with line. Thus if we listen to a single tone, it is relatively unlikely to lead to an aesthetic occasion, first, because there is so little kinaesthesis in this perceptual situation, and, second, because such activity as there is does not lend itself to simplification and completion. It is worth observing in this connection that performing artists rarely strike tones exactly on pitch. It is customary, especially on the violin, to strike the tone a little

41

below pitch and come up to exact pitch, for this change is one which involves more activity in perception, and especially an activity which involves completion. Through this forming activity the tone as content comes to be revealed.

Similarly to the sounding of single tones, the drawing of perfectly straight lines baffles successful completion of kinaesthetic activity; there are no ends capable of being reached either by the artist or the appreciator, and so their parts fail to be brought into relation with one another. By contrast a curving line is more often simple and completable in the technical sense in which these terms are used here; that is, such a line, as drawn or perceived, involves activity which leads into the emergence of content. Indeed, the activity of forming implicit in curving lines is especially able to reveal content. This activity has the characteristic of being a simple and completable sequence of acts, and so of being capable of forming content. In consequence a curving line enfolds its points, and it discloses as well the areas adjacent to the line, particularly those held in the curve. The movement which sweeps out the curves is a sequence of simple and completable acts providing entry into a partially enclosed space, into the texture of paper and paint. The points brought into relation by the line, the space, the paper, and the paint which the curve enfolds emerge in the art-work as disclosed content.

IV. *Figure, Symmetry, and Realm*

The sweep of a curving line may become a figure; at least a line which is developed to cross itself may build a figure, and certainly the interweaving of two lines does evolve a figure. In order to evolve out of aesthetic lines a figure requires more than simple and completable activity, it requires an activity of forming which can be carried through in different ways. From the perspective of the artist, his artistic activities generate the possibilities of alternative paths as they reflect his decisions to proceed in this way rather than that in the development of a figure. The artwork which he develops leads into a content formed by these possibilities, a space of possibilities which holds variegated content in a dynamic net. As appreciators we develop lines into figures in a variety of ways, and there is tentativeness in this development as we decide between alternative routes equally open to us. The acts by which we develop a figure and come to envision it, although simple and successfully completed in one sequence, may be completed in different ways. Over a period of aesthetic activity they often are completed in many ways. A figure, actively envisioned, enfolds area, as does a line; but its development also generates the space of possibilities which reveals more richly the texture of paper or canvas, the solidity of paints, the reality of color and represented object as these are held within the balance of alternative forms. This variety characterizes an aesthetic activity which leads into richer aesthetic occasions.

The development of a true geometrical figure is rather rare in an art-work. As the advantage of a curving line over a straight running line is the advantage of an aesthetic participation which leads into an aesthetic occasion, so the figure developed by the artist is usually freely drawn just because a freely developing pattern involves aesthetic activity which leads into variegated disclosed content.

Such content is held in the net of possibilities which a freely evolving pattern formulates. The artist avoids sketching the true circle and prefers some less regular construction just because the true circle affords, in the movement of creation, no real alternatives for aesthetic activity. The true circle also impresses the appreciator as static, since in his development of it alternative paths of activity are not held in balance. The introduction of repeated figures into the development of an art-work often has a similar deadening effect. The construction of a repeated pattern often reduces aesthetic activity to perfunctory movement, for the repetition prevents incorporation of a sense of alternative movements in the activity. To an appreciator such repetitious activity seems artificial, dull, and dead because it leads nowhere. It seems monotonous because it terminates in the repeated patterns rather than carrying through these to an emerging content.

Of course, repetition is not the only way in which patterning may be developed to call attention to form rather than to lead into aesthetic occasions. One may so artfully arrange drapery that one's activity is preoccupied with the pattern of the folds and obscures the material and its texture. Such development of pattern is often called decorative: it adorns; it comes to be, not to reveal, but for its own sake. Yet the development of figure through patterning need not fail to lead into an aesthetic occasion. Patterning activity, properly carried through, can be aesthetic activity disclosing content, as it is, for example, in the appreciation of some Chinese ceramics. Here appreciative response builds a figure of possibilities, of recognized alternative paths of movement from the stem, leaf, flower,

44

and color design of the vase; a figure in which the clay of the vase, the glaze, indeed, the represented flowers emerge in a great variety of ways.

A living figure is one in which the activities of creation or appreciation of elements (themselves actively grasped) and their relations comprise a plurality of paths along which development and response occur, and so a way of forming which reveals an exceptional variety and richness of content. We call such a living figure *symmetrical*: it involves a dynamic balance of alternative paths of movement leading into an aesthetic occasion. Symmetry is a balance of movement in the art-work which accords to content the dynamic frame contributing to its emergence in manifold ways.

The development of symmetry in an art-work leads into an aesthetic occasion within the dynamic balance of alternative paths disclosing content. Such dynamic balance in the art-work suggests the forming of content in a variety of ways, but, more important, evokes a sense of ever greater possibilities of disclosing content. In symmetry the activity of artist or appreciator is developed as completable but never completed, so that we are aware of it as continuously terminating in an aesthetic occasion. Symmetry in an art-work not only qualifies activity so that there is a continuous evocation of a manifold of formed content; it also suggests, if weakly, that such activity participates in a continuously developing aesthetic occasion. When this occurs we speak of the living quality of art. Symmetry, that is, suggests that there is a *realm* in which there is not only a rich manifold of disclosed content, but a movement in which the continuous articulation of content occurs.

The suggestion of a realm may be achieved in an art-work in other ways than through that development of line into the dynamic balance of figure we have called symmetry. Certainly there are aesthetic activities relating to music and poetry which may serve this function. By analogy we may develop the line of a melody into the balanced pattern of musical phrases, or the rhymes of poetry into the dynamic balance of a sonnet. In the case of these and the other arts as well, the artist's activity develops an art-work in which his actions (and subsequently those of the appreciator) terminate in disclosing content, serve, that is, as a path opening to an aesthetic occasion and making this occasion accessible. Such a movement along a path within the art-work allows content to emerge within the activity of forming, to be essentially articulated by form, to become a part of an ultimate process made up of form *and* content. But more than this, disclosure of content through the activity of a forming which possesses symmetry evokes the possibility of a continuing emergence of content and its articulation. This possibility is suggested in the movement of the opaque immediacy of the given, forth to disclosure and back into opaque givenness as this movement is reiterated in symmetry. The complex activity of forming involved in symmetry suggests, if only weakly, that this reiterated movement is a developing articulation of content, a realm.

Let us turn to some examples of such suggestion. We turn to them figuratively only, since our words can refer but indirectly to the art-work. First, let us consider a poorly baked pot picked up in a Paris street market, and designed for the purpose of holding salt, or, perhaps, a small flower or two. Imagine the pot to be about two and one-half inches in height. It has a rim and a small pouring lip. It is made of reddish clay and has some sort of an indifferent glaze. When we look into the pot from the top we may respond aesthetically and develop a circular sweep based on the outside rim and evolve a series of concentric circles based on the inside wall as we develop its slopes inward toward the bottom. Or, looked at from the side our aesthetic response may ascend and expand, since the pot is smaller at the bottom than at the top, and may come to balance in a development of the cylinder of clay which forms the rim. Thus if our aesthetic response carries us into an art-work, it may do so through the activity of developing imperfect circular forms. The inspiration to imperfect forming in this case rests in the fact that the potter made no effort to come close to a geometrical standard. And this imperfection in the art-object may be carried over into the evolution of other figures, into developing a section of the cylinder comprising the rim, the part of the cone comprising the sides, and the plane of the bottom. If these figures evolve, the balance attained in them may afford an intuition, a disclosure, of the reddish color of the clay, or alternatively the baked-in hardness of the pot, or again, its earthen solidity. Thus a variety of content emerges in the imperfect, in the accidental symmetry attained. Through this accidental symmetry the glaze comes to have an area over which it spreads and penetrates into the clay so that we are admitted to an intuition of this earth.

One of the characteristics of the symmetry in an art-work based upon this insignificant pot is its apparently accidental attainment. The dynamic balance developed on the basis of such an imperfect art-object as this is tentative; the content disclosed is various, depending upon the momentary and shifting focus of the aesthetic response. Thus the symmetry attained is a kind of instability in the art-work, an instability which has the effect of shifting forms unexpectedly and resulting in the disclosure of one aspect of content and then another. Thus the very imperfection of the art-object results in an instability in the art-work which leads into a manifold of disclosed content.

It is the awareness of imperfection in the art-object and the sense of the instability comprising the symmetry developed in the art-work which suggest, if weakly, the possibility of continued evocation of emerging content. The sense of this continued evocation, this adumbration of a realm, is to be found in our awareness that this art-object, this pot, could collapse into the opaque earth from whence it came; that the instability comprising the symmetry attained in this art-work could dissolve back into the elements of form whose precarious balance so insecurely comprises it. The imperfection and instability in this situation enable us to grasp the fact that the continued articulation of content, a realm, requires more support than is available here; and through this sense of a lack we are able to grasp the significance of a realm.

The adumbration of a realm in the case of better art than the poorly baked pot we have been considering, can hardly occur through such lacks as imperfection and instability. In better art the relative perfection of the art-object precludes the attainment of symmetry in instability. A good Meissen vase may comprise relatively perfect ele-

48

ments which can be interrelated and developed into symmetry; yet when this happens the balance achieved must be a positive one. Aesthetic response to the lines and colors of the designs of such a vase comes to differentiate the porcelain, revealing fine texture, hardness, and impermeability. Response to the curves and surfaces of the porcelain discloses in turn the lines and colors of the designs. The glazed colors of the vase, the highlights of its surfaces, hold in reflection something of the content of the surroundings in which the vase stands. Here the dynamic balance of symmetry reaches a high order, disclosing a rich manifold of content. But in the movement of this dynamic balance disclosing content there is little other than the reiteration of the movement to suggest that there could be a continuing emergence of content, a process in which content is continuously articulated. Where the complex movement of symmetry is rich enough to stand in its own right, where we do not sense this movement as based on imperfection and instability, there is little adumbration of the realm of art. If, however, the movement of disclosure achieved in symmetry may only hint at entry into a realm in which there is a continuous articulation of content, there are other forms making this clearer; and it is our next task to determine what they are and how they serve this end.

CHAPTER 3

REFLEXIVE FORMS

I. *Human Meaning and Value in Art: Expression*

A statue of a dancer or an abstract arrangement of metal rods may express lightness and poise. A song or a melody may express gaiety. A dance may convey a sense of soaring. The patterns of a drawing may express melancholy. In these and other cases what is expressed is implicit and immediate; it is expressed directly, it is presented. But a statue of a dancer represents a dancer, a song may describe a gay scene, a drawing may be of a melancholy circumstance. Often enough a poem begins as does the ballad "Fair Margaret and Sweet William":

> As it fell out on a long summer's
>   day
> Two lovers they sat on a hill;

In such a case the rhythm, meter, and sounds of the words seem to present us with a mood which the represented scene also conveys.

The Rospiglioso Cup, attributed to Benvenuto Cellini, expresses great richness. In the cup we are presented with a variety of bright color intensified in enamel work. The shapes are extravagant; the use of ornaments of jewels is lavish. Indeed, the mermaid is adorned with an impressive baroque pearl suspended as a pendulum from her throat. And a veritable pot-pourri of represented figures and objects from myth and tradition, all carrying value tones for us in consequence of their representative significance, are comprised in the Cup. Thus a golden cup rests upon the wings of a dragon which, in turn, stands upon the back of a tortoise. The form of the cup is a shell, and on the hinge of the shell rests a mermaid. The materials and elements expressing varieties of richness by immediate presentation and by representation are evident enough.

Of course an artist may reduce the extent of representation in an art-work, or even eliminate it entirely. Thus an artist who engages in abstract sculpturing may avoid introducing into the art-work he develops any patterning activities which have representative significance. The activities involved in representing a natural object, the human figure or head, or indeed, any recognizable object may be eliminated from sculpting without difficulty. Yet when the artist does this it is usually clear enough that his intention is to make a place for presented values, in particular those expressed by lines and shapes, masses and textures, and materials. The sculptor handles and forms his materials in order to express values directly, that is, without representing anything. By doing so he enhances presented values such as harshness or softness, weight or lightness, intricacy or simplicity and makes them much more central to the art-work. Similarly, it is possible for a poet to write a poem telling no story, depicting no recognizable emotion, using no words or phrases symbolizing known objects or circumstances. Yet when this is done, or even when it is done to some extent, it usually permits the rhyme and rhythm, the metrical pattern, the tones and sounds of words and syllables to express value more directly than can be done in conventional poetry.

The media and structures of art are things to which men respond affectively, as their expression of presented values

52

shows. Clearly an artist whose reactions to his medium were negative could not work in it effectively, nor could an appreciator who disliked sounds, for example, hope to develop an art-work based upon music. What could an architect do who was not enamored of stone and glass and steel, who felt no joy in the interrelation of volumes and planes of space, who was not interested in the uses to which buildings are put and their general function in human society? What could a poet achieve who was psychologically indifferent to rhythms, meters, words? . . . who was not elated by the occurrence of chance rhyme and turns of phrase? Such a "poet" would find the character of his medium so opaque that he could not begin to work with it. But the artist who responds positively to his medium carries his love and delight over into it in his own terms. The way in which he handles his medium expresses not only his care for it, but other aspects of his personality as well. The selection he makes of values to present and subject-matter to represent tell an appreciator a great deal about the artist. In fact, because of the yielding nature of the medium and the ease of selection of values and subject-matter he is often able to express himself with a greater degree of coherence and clarity than is possible outside of art. No doubt one of the attractions of art for the artist is just this, and when such self-expression is achieved this becomes an attraction for an appreciator as well. The artist is often an interesting man, and the expression of his personality through his selection of materials and the techniques he uses can be fascinating.

It is a fact, too, that the artist expresses not only his own temper, interests, and values, but those of his times and culture. The artist's choice of medium, presented values, and represented subjects, and his handling of these may be peculiarly his own, but they are conditioned by his education and the tastes of his times: something which the classification of art-objects by periods makes clear enough. In representational art, especially, the choice of theme and the manner of interpretation usually reflect a social matrix, as we may see if we compare, say, a tragedy of Sophocles with a novel of Tolstoi. We are aware, too, that patterns of certain cultures were especially closely related to the art-forms which they supported: the drama in ancient Greece and Elizabethan England, the novel in 19th century Russia, painting in renaissance Italy. When we find vitality, love of variety, indifference to intellectual rigor expressed in a play, for example, this is an expression of cultural predilections as often as of merely personal temper.

The expression in art of some aspects of the history and complex society of which we are a part can catch our attention. We are interested in human history and culture, and the mirror art holds up to them is often a good one. Art is often able to express central values and typical events of an epoch with a clarity and concreteness they cannot have even as lived. Art contributes to our understanding of history and life.

Certainly many people are concerned with art in such terms as those we have been discussing; their response to art-objects terminates in expression. Many people dwell upon the values presented in the art-object, or find the clarity and concreteness of represented subject-matter a real contribution to its comprehension. Many people are fascinated by the free and unitary expression of the artist's personality in art, and by what they find reflected in art of the spirit and significance of an epoch. But responses to art-objects which terminate in expression are often aesthetic activities as well. We may see something more of the integral relation of expression to an art-work by noting one function of the expression of richness in the case of the Rospiglioso Cup. This sense of richness is evoked by materials and objects relating to our valuing of wealth, something we have learned to do because of the practical importance of wealth in both our personal experience and human history generally. The expression of richness in art is based upon materials and elements associated with practical lessons and calls for responses which, initially at least, have to do with success and position. For this reason the Rospiglioso Cup communicates to a wide audience, for most people respond positively to its richness.

This is not to say that such positive response is external to art. Quite the contrary, it serves in this case, at least, to develop an art-work and so to lead into an aesthetic occasion. Our initial response to the Rospiglioso Cup in terms of richness somehow carries back into the elaborateness of line and curve, into the flamboyance of surface, and from these into the texture and color of the gold and jewels and enamel. The representation of tortoise, dragon, mermaid, and sea-shell helps in some way to develop response via line and pattern, and to lead to the content of texture, color, and material. The vital personality of the artist and the unrestrained character of his times which interest us initially have the peculiar effect of bringing our responses gradually to a focus in relation to that disclosure of content which is the heart of an art-work. Nor is this to say that expression is reduced to the elements of an art-work discussed in Chapter Two, that is, to the disclosure of content in and by line, figure, and symmetry. Rather, it is to suggest that the disclosure of content in the art-work differs as a result of the creative or responsive activities involved in expression. What is peculiar to the disclosure of content in which expression plays an integral part must now be examined.

II. *Forming by Contrast and Function: Inception*

We observed in Chapter One that the dominance of human preoccupation with extra-aesthetic functions of art may draw a veil across it; but that by the more or less deliberate use of certain artistic devices, such as rhythm and stress in poetry and their analogues in other arts, the artist may succeed in rending this veil. We observed, too, that when this happens a new relation between man and art is established which alters man's nature. It is true as well that extra-aesthetic values which art-objects have and express distract from art, so long as response to these is in their terms; but that they may be used in such a way as to provide access to an aesthetic occasion. When this is done apparently nonaesthetic values come to contribute to the development of the art-work and the disclosure of content occurring in it. How the extra-aesthetic values of art may be used in this way and the significance of such use for disclosing content we have now to determine in detail.

Let us consider to begin with the most evident ways in which economic value may be related to the disclosure of content in an art-work. Perhaps the simplest obvious example of economic value developing an art-work is to be found in the significance of the cost of tickets to an artistic performance. We may buy the most expensive seats in the house, but it is not often that we put the matter in exactly this way. Normally, we think of seats as oriented toward the performance (as they are) and so as an important if somewhat remote means to the end of participating in an art-work. In consequence we say we have "the best seats in the house," a phrase which formulates economic value in relation to art. What is comprised in this somewhat literal figure is that awareness of economic value arrests us and focuses our attention, and that we come to focus our attention upon the performance rather than upon the cost. Such use of economic value to highlight the art-object and promote participation in the art-work may be found in explicit reference to the cost of the art-object in such a way, for example, as to indicate that it is priceless. Thus the Metropolitan Museum of New York City noted, in a display of a pair of Chinese ceramic statues of the K'ang-hsi period, that at one time John D. Rockefeller, Jr., owned one and Harry E. Widener the other. Since the pair belonged together, several attempts were made by Rockefeller and Widener to negotiate a sale of one statue, but fruitlessly. Finally, Rockefeller acquired both by winning on the toss of a coin. By implication, the statues are in fact priceless; and the viewer is asked to take this arresting economic fact into account and then to transfer his focused attention to the end of a careful examination of the objects, and presumably a deeper involvement in an art-work.

Clearly, other human values such as comfort and social intercourse can be used in such a way as to contribute to development of an art-work. Talk before the curtain or during an intermission may be brought to bear upon a performance, and may aid in relating to it. Actually, in some cases, the whole range of extra-aesthetic human preoccupations may be used as a propaedeutic to involvement in the art-work. One approaches the town of Chartres from Paris through a penumbra of human meanings spread out across the countryside in the patterns of typical French life and culture. And as one nears the town, the cathedral there appears, at the end of the road across the plain of Beauce, as a spire emerging from the earth on the distant horizon. The movement through the patterns of human culture, as we become aware of it, comes to have the significance of a path leading toward the cathedral, and so serves to focus our attention more sharply upon the art-object which is the goal of the movement. This focus sparks our aesthetic response and involves us in the startling beginning of disclosure of content in an art-work.

No doubt this beginning is the result of a happy accident of terrain, but this accident contributes to the intention of the builders. We may see this if we note that the same effect is obtained in consequence of the location of the cathedral in the town. There the cathedral is placed in the midst of nonaesthetic patterns and values in such a way that these may be used to set off its radically different lines, forms, and architectural structures; that is, they provide, if we use them in this way, the contrast which establishes the subliminal presence of the art-object and so the basis for a shift of attention through ordinary human pre-occupations to the cathedral. We may note the basis for this shift of attention in contrast by approaching the cathedral and entering it. Standing in the small park at the rear one need not be immersed in religious meaning but may be aware only of the existence of a cathedral in a religious tradition one knows and understands, and one's attention may be rather startlingly shifted out of this awareness to focus in the intricate spatial relations and the living patterns of the flying buttresses. Approaching the cathedral from the front or the side, one may be caught initially by the fact of the depictions of one or the other parts of the Christian myth in the reliefs; or standing in the nave or choir one may be aware of their service in the life of the church and the significance for religious mean-ing of the sculptured scenes from the Christian tradition found there. The setting of the town and the religious meanings which are a part of the cathedral can be used to provide a contrast with and so to help shift attention to the forms of the arches and the complex interrelation of volumes of space which catch one up in the developing art-work, and lead into a disclosure of content *having a beginning*.

This shift of attention and its singular effect upon dis-closure of content can occur not only as a result of viewing extra-aesthetic values in contrast to the art-object; but, for another example, it can also take place as a consequence of what is ordinarily called functional design. Here, as for instance in functional architecture, the design follows function, and our attention comes to focus upon design as fit for the human function of the building. In such design, function is no longer viewed as related to man's need but relates to the art-object; and attention, initially focused in function, comes to rest in the art-object and so comes to aid development of an art-work. The shapes and surfaces of an airplane which enable it to function effectively for air transport are also the forms of an art-object, and when seen in this light evoke a response which leads through the art-work into disclosure of content. The shift of attention from function to its existence as form in an art-object gives to the disclosure of content, when it occurs, a moment of inception, a beginning.

In those examples given, in which economic value, religious significance, or a congeries of human values are related to the art-work by being viewed as in contrast or as functional design, the relation may seem quite external. Indeed, it must seem evident that many instances of a closer relation can be found. The use of ivory and gold as the material for a figurine evidently carries the economic value of the material into the warmth and richness of tone which the statuette evokes in our response to it. The sense of religious mystery to be found in the darkened recesses of the vaulted space of a cathedral seems to be held in that space itself. The pleasant intricacy of the complex but precise pattern of the shapes of a supersonic fighter seems to be the expression of its geometry more than a property of the function of these shapes in flight. But these and the many other similar instances are not the best illustrations of the point now in question. The examples we have chosen are just those in which the relation of extra-aesthetic values to the art-work characterizes disclosure of content as having a beginning. This characterization can occur when human values are recognized as existing in relation to other elements in an art-work through, for example, the use of contrast with its potential for a shift of attention to the art-object, or, more positively, by treating them as the ends for functional design which binds them directly to the art-object.

To a considerable extent involvement in an art-work by an artist or an appreciator may take place without explicit characterization of the aesthetic occasion, in which such involvement terminates, as having a beginning. Indeed, the analysis of Chapter Two was developed without any explicit reference to this property. To the extent that participation takes place without this reference being made explicit, the disclosure of content in an art-work must seem a miracle, and the relevance of the activities of forming to it must seem a mystery. Yet the activities of forming involved in an art-work always appear to some extent, say to the artist, as opening a path leading into an aesthetic occasion. It is the function of the relation of extra-aesthetic values to the art-work by means, say, of contrast or functional design to make the fact of this contribution explicit, and to constitute a kind of forming in their own right. When this forming takes place effectively, it modifies radically the disclosure of content, characterizing the aesthetic occasion as having an *inception,* giving to its occurrence in the art-work an explicit beginning.

Aesthetic intuition, the participation in an aesthetic occasion, is not something which simply happens to man. When the contributive activities of forming as found in line, figure, or symmetry, for example, develop an art-work and lead into an aesthetic occasion, this occurs as a consequence of an implicit orientation of human nature. However, when extra-aesthetic values are introduced into an art-work by intention, and when their peculiarly human character is emphasized by setting them in contrast or in functional relation to, say, line, figure, and symmetry; then there is a demand, framed within the art-work, for the implicit contribution of human nature to the aesthetic occasion to be made explicit. It is the artist (or appreciator) involved in the art-work who must develop or respond to this demand. If he does not respond the extra-aesthetic values will close the way to the aesthetic occasion by dominating the experience. But if, for example, under the impact of sharp contrast of these values with peculiarly aesthetic elements, or the relation of these values to aesthetic elements in functional design, he recognizes the possibility of developing an art-work as a contributor, he accepts as well the need to immerse human nature in an aesthetic occasion and the transmutation of that nature implied by this immersion. It is the inception of such a transmutation which is reflected in the fact that, where this forming is effective, participation in disclosed content is participation in an aesthetic occasion having a beginning. For this reason we call the forming activities such as those involving contrast and functional design *reflexive forming*.

To say that an aesthetic occasion has a beginning is to refer to the recognition that the disclosing of content is, in part, a consequence of the contribution by the participator of his own nature to the art-work. From the perspective of the contributor this appears initially as an orientation toward the art-work, and then as an involvement in this. To the contributor there is a focusing of his powers followed by an embedding of his activity in the developing art-work. We have noted that this focusing of the contributor's powers takes place through contrast and functional design and becomes the inception of an aesthetic occasion. We have seen how this inception depends upon introducing human values and meanings into a context where other elements preclude their domination; where, in fact, other elements in the art-work set a limit to human nature, give to it a boundary, and so function to demand its orientation to what is beyond the merely the contributor's powers takes place through contrast and functional design, formulates a significance of human nature in the art-work as the beginning of the aesthetic occasion. But human nature has other significance for the aesthetic occasion: it also serves to sustain its otherwise fugitive nature.

III. Forming by Exfoliation: Presence

Some of us expend a great deal of effort analyzing and trying to fix the themes of art, wondering what meanings the artist wanted to evoke and what meanings he did evoke. We often look to art for wisdom, arguing sometimes that art communicates better than anything else, saying that the deepest insights into man and his condition are to be found there. Certainly art which uses language clearly cannot avoid representing and conveying meaning, whatever else may be involved. In *Moby Dick* we learn something about whaling and about evil; in

Eugénie Grandet we find the evocation of a pure character in the midst of French provincial society; *Les Misérables* conveys a sense of a unity which transcends the variety and evils it holds within it. The use of words in literature makes the carrying of this sort of meaning inevitable; but most art carries meaning in a similar way.

In literature, communication of meaning often occurs in the form of short essays or didactic passages introduced into a novel or a poem. When this happens we assess the significance of literature in terms of its expressed moral, noetic, or practical value. Such an assessment is hardly avoidable in the case of literature; but even here one can ask whether this assessment of subject-matter does not separate the subject from its essential aesthetic matrix and so make the evaluation aesthetically irrelevant.

The issue is clearest, perhaps, in relation to music where it may be argued that subject-matter in the sense in which it is to be found in literature does not exist at all. A writer needs something to write about; he needs to understand his subject, even to have a strong emotional orientation to it in order to write effectively. The situation in the composition of music is not very similar to this, for composition does not require an explicit subject. Still, many composers program their music. Beethoven, in his *Pastoral Symphony*, tells us the emotional content of each of the sections by using such headings as: "The awakening of cheerful feelings on arriving in the country"; "Merry making of country folk"; "Thunderstorm, tempest"; "Song of the shepherds. Glad and thankful feelings after the storm." If we read the program to a performance, or if we have read the score, we know what emotions and imagery

Beethoven expects us to feel upon hearing his music. It is only up to us to respond according to his directions. Richard Strauss goes even further in *Till Eulenspiegel*. He sets the emotional tone of the music by telling us that it depicts the story of a legendary mischievous boy in medieval Germany, so that we expect to be and are amused, surprised, and delighted. But Strauss also tells us he has built into the music specific pranks, such as Till riding horseback into a crowd of women at the market, disguising himself as a priest, hiding in a mouse hole, and finally, being caught, tried, and hanged—even to the final squeal on the gallows. These directions ask us to imagine the events in some detail on the occasion of certain musical phrases.

It is true that in music thus programmed one can and often does follow the directions of the composer; so that one contributes the suggested emotions and imagery as requested. It is also true, however, that if one has never heard a piece of music and does not read the composer's program before hearing it, the response is very likely, almost inevitably, quite wide of the composer's suggestions. People curious about this matter have shown repeatedly that listeners unfamiliar with musical compositions not only respond to the performance with emotions and imagery quite different from that the composer thought to be appropriate, but that they also evidence no pattern of agreement among themselves. Uninstructed listeners find no predictable emotions or imaginative scenes corresponding to the musical phrases as such, even when they do say that their response is emotional and imaginative. Are we, then, to say that emotional response to musical phrase is arbitrary? That imaginative response to music is uncontrolled by the music itself?

If a composer does not program his music, we find this acceptable and respond after our own fashion. Thus Rachmaninoff has not told us what to feel or imagine in response to the *Prelude in C-sharp minor*, leaving us free to respond as we please. Is not one implication of this freedom to be found in a rule requiring a distinction between music proper and the sort of free response we make to it? Ought we not, so far as we are interested in music, focus our attention upon motive and phrase and the way development is introduced via tonality and section? Ought we not, that is, speak of Rachmaninoff's *Prelude* as a development of a descending melodic figure of three notes of equal value? And by implication disregard emotion and imagination? There is always something attractive in making a step toward objectivity, in picking out something on which general agreement can be reached. Perhaps we can agree that the motive of the *Prelude* is comprised of three notes, and that its development occurs in three sections, of which the second provides a weaker statement based on a related four note figure. Yet, having said this, or something like this in the case of other musical compositions, have we really resolved the issue? Musical motives and phrases are often parts of folk melodies, and focusing attention upon them out of this context seems unlikely to divorce them completely from the emotional and imaginative significance they have in it. The history of discussions of the nature of music is filled with argument over the meaning of tonality and its relation to the ability of music to express, as well as a consideration of the variation in tonality from one age to the next.

The point of the relation of emotion and image to music, or, more generally, presentative or representative meaning to art, tends to be missed if it is formulated as a problem of whether this is, in fact, an "objective" relation. Such an intellectual formulation neglects the fact that meaning is an aspect of the dynamic complex which is the art-work. We do better when we hold this fact centrally within our attention by speaking of the developing art-work as flowering into a variety of meanings. To say this is to refer to the way in which aesthetic intuition bursts into multiple emotions and a plenum of images, to take account of the movement disclosing content as breaking into a myriad of patterns and facets of meaning. Thus, at least, we are open to the mystery of the relation of meaning to art. This mystery inheres in the emergence of meanings having a part to play in the disclosure of content, a part they play not in terms of their explicit reference or ostensible signification; but in the evidence they afford that disclosure of content may be a continuous movement of articulation. The forming activities involved in disclosure of content not only involve a contribution of man, but this contribution can be continued and the disclosure maintained. This evidence is to be found, for example, when motive and melody, tonality and polyphony in a musical composition are strained and pulled to burgeon into a multiplicity of ambiguous suggestions of meanings, for then we sense the disclosure of content in an art-work not only as having a beginning, but as continuing: as having *presence*.

In discussing inception we noted that the effectiveness of this forming depends upon the introduction of human value into a context where its ostensible significance contrasts with other elements in the art-work. When this is done these elements serve to set a bound to man's nature, and so they make explicit the fact that this nature may be oriented toward what lies beyond it in such a way as to contribute to the disclosure of content. The existence of this orientation is made explicit in an art-work, first, as the beginning of an aesthetic occasion. The significance of this orientation may extend, second, to include the presence of an aesthetic occasion; that is, disclosure of content as continuous articulation.

Let us call the meanings introduced into an art-work in this second way and for this second purpose *symbolic*. Thus the emotions and imagery evoked in an art-work by the tones, motives, melodies, rhythms, and organizing patterns of music may be symbolic if their very polyvalence relates them to the relative opacity of the underlying music in such a way as to bring this to the fore, to give it presence. This complex use of meanings in an art-work needs illustration, and an example from poetry can serve us best. We know that poetry is built up of complex patterns of sound. In this there is a resemblance to music. But by taking a poem as an example, it will be possible to deal with the art-object itself in our discussion, something not possible in the case of music. The patterns of sounds and rhythms in poetry serve to originate a movement into an aesthetic occasion; but the words and phrases may also introduce symbolic meanings. This is something of which the artist is aware, for he introduces meanings in special ways in relation to the sounds and rhythms carrying them. We see such ways in which meanings are introduced in the poem William Blake called "The Tiger."

68

THE TIGER

Tiger! Tiger! burning bright
In the forests of the night,
What immortal hand or eye
Could frame thy fearful symmetry?

In what distant deeps or skies
Burnt the fire of thine eyes?
On what wings dare he aspire?
What the hand dare seize the fire?

And what shoulder, and what art,
Could twist the sinews of thy heart?
And when thy heart began to beat
What dread hand? and what dread feet?

What the hammer? what the chain?
In what furnace was thy brain?
What the anvil? what dread grasp
Dare its deadly terrors clasp?

When the stars threw down their spears,
And water'd heaven with their tears,
Did he smile his work to see?
Did he who made the Lamb make thee?

Tiger! Tiger! burning bright
In the forests of the night,
What immortal hand or eye,
Dare frame thy fearful symmetry?

This poem is of especial interest as an illustration of that expressive forming we have called presence. The poem not only exemplifies this presence, but it is also a poem in which the poet is explicitly concerned with a theme very similar to the idea of presence, that is, the relation of creature to creation. We have said that where presence occurs in an art-work there is a movement explicitly articulating relatively concealed content. This situation is mirrored by Blake's presentation of the creature as somehow reflecting its ground in creation; that is, as emerging in the mysterious context of creation, as an articulation of this ground. Blake presents a developing statement of meanings of increasing intricacy which he complicates to the point where even the extending variety and subtlety of these meanings can be seen to fail, at the level of language, in the task of articulation undertaken. He treats this failure, not as absolute, but as shifting attention from the goal of the struggle toward articulation back to the source and ground of this struggle in creation; something which as appreciators we can follow in the language as a shift from a developing kaleidoscope of meanings to the rhymes, rhythms, and patterns of sounds in the poem. For the sake of clarity we focus our analysis of this presentation on images, as one instance of meaning.

In the first two lines of the poem, Blake presents the reader with three images. The first is the tiger; the second is that of the tiger burning bright; and the last that of the tiger burning in the forests of the night. The first image is quite ordinary, if emphatic. The second image is imaginative, and we are told that the tiger is like a flame; but since he is not exactly like a flame our imaginations must move to probe this likeness in difference. We may imagine the orange of his fur as flame against the black. We may imagine the tiger's eyes burning as do a cat's eyes in the dark. Or we may imagine him burning with energy in a spring, or moving as quickly as a wandering flame through the forest. In any case, the variety of emergent meanings comprises a movement toward the vision of the tiger, giving it depth and significance, and suggesting an articulation of the creature's unity. The third image is polyvalent as presented, for the forests of the night must be comprehended by imaginative response before one can put a tiger into them. The night is literally dark; but it is also nothing and inscrutable. So, since the forests are those of the night, we may imagine them not merely as the trees made up of the black stripes of the tiger, but as an image of the ambiguous structure of the night, and thus, enchanted forests. But then we must see the tiger moving in the enchanted forest, and enchanted too; and as we shall see, a symbol. And the fire becomes enchanted, and a symbol.

The question Blake asks next, "What immortal hand or eye could frame thy fearful symmetry?" is intended to help fix these symbols. It is a question which can be asked only because the "fearful symmetry" has been established as fearful in the sense of awesome as well as fearsome. We fear the tiger, of course. The awesomeness of the tiger which is like the awesomeness of God has been established by the location of the tiger within an enchanted forest. In consequence, the tiger comes to symbolize the *emerging* creature, and the fire the *living flame* of creation, behind which stands the creator.

In the next three stanzas Blake develops the relation of creature to creation by a further multiplication of meanings and image. In part this development is presented in straightforward elaboration of images portraying the creature's creator in human form. "What the hand dare seize the fire? And what shoulder, and what art, Could twist the sinews of thy heart?" But, in part, the intent of these images is to be misleading since, clearly, the creator in this case is not of human form, so that the similarity is stated only to be qualified. It is qualified by the questions, which suggest differences between man and the creator; indeed, the questions are phrased to suggest differences so great as to deny the similarity initially portrayed. To ask, "what shoulder, and what art" is to intimate that there could be none in the usual sense, so that the image is to be understood in some more complex sense. To ask, "what the hand dare seize the fire?" is, again, to introduce the suggestion that there could be no *hand* so daring. Yet we know that creation burns in the fire of the tiger's eye. We have, thus, lines in which the explicit nature of the creature is attributed to its fabrication after the fashion of human artifice; but which, at the same time, suggest that creation takes place in some radically different way.

Blake does not stop here. He goes on to use full irrelevance and confusion to force still stronger paradox, and so to remove the image of an anthropomorphic creation. The third line of the second stanza, "On what wings dare he aspire?" is very odd; it should refer to the tiger's creator, and yet the suggestion has been that this is God. But God need not, can not aspire; so we shift our interpretation to entertain the idea that "he" is the tiger. And perhaps the creature does aspire. Yet the confusing ambiguity of this line remains. As it happens, the manuscript draft (see page 187) contains an alternate and clearer second stanza:

> Burnt in distant deeps or skies
> The cruel fire of thine eyes
> Could heart descend or wings aspire
> What the hand dare seize the fire?

In this version the third line more clearly implies that the creator is not similar to man, for the ambiguous suggestion is that heart could not descend nor wings aspire toward the creator. And this negation of any similarity to human competence is underlined by the suggestion in the last line that nothing like a human hand dare seize the fire.

Blake did not use the clearer alternative stanza, preferring to introduce an ambiguous line. That this is intentional we see from the last line of the third stanza, which is also ambiguous. "What dread hand? and what dread feet?" may refer to the hand of the creator; but the feet to which it refers could be those of the creator or of the tiger—we are not told enough to decide. Above all, we are caught up by this line through not knowing what these feet, to whomever they belong, are doing. The introduction of such a line relates creator to creature *and* obscures the nature of the relation.

The manuscript draft of the poem reveals to us the deliberateness of the artist's use of this obscurity, for in it there is a stanza following the third stanza of the finished poem which tells us whose feet these are and what they are doing. This is:

> . . . and what dread feet?
>
> Could fetch it from the furnace deep
> And in thy horrid ribs dare steep
> In the well of sanguine woe
> In what clay & in what mould
> Were the eyes of fury rolld

The addition of this stanza to the poem makes the hands and feet those of the creator who fetches the heart from the deep furnace. Yet the poet excised this stanza and with it the clarity it affords. It is interesting to note that Blake permitted publication of one variant of the line we are discussing, the last line of the third stanza. In Dr. Malkin's *Father's Memoirs of his Child*, presumably approved by Blake, the line in question reads "What dread hand forged thy dread feet." This removes the ambiguity; but the poet permitted this clearer version only once, preferring to suggest an intellectually opaque relation of creature to creator.

To understand this line and the slightly less difficult third line of the second stanza, "On what wings dare he aspire?," requires an acceptance of the poet's intention to introduce ambiguity, or less paradoxically put, perhaps, to relate the creature back to the mystery of creation. Blake handles this task in the poem by mirroring the issue at the level of language. Beginning with imaged similarities between tigers and fire, which entail dissimilarities as well, he goes on to similarities and differences between tigers

74

and fire in an enchanted forest. This he does by the straightforward use of language to evoke image, and he multiplies images by a moderate use of ambiguity of word and phrase. He proceeds, next, to present the tiger as a symbol of the creature and fire as a symbol of creation, emphasizing the particularity of the creature by the metaphor of a creator in human form who constructs a specific creature. The content of this metaphor, that the particularity of the creature is a product of a kind of human fabrication, is duplicated in the creation of the language by the poet; here too the construction of the poem suggests *the* specific articulation of underlying strands and images. But the explicitness of the relation of creature to creator which is both the content of the metaphor and part of the poet's use of language, is misleading; it focuses attention upon the product and screens the nature of the process which is integral to this result. Blake avoids this explicitness and tries to reestablish something of the mystery of creation–creature by deliberately avoiding clarity in language, even by removing clarifying phrases and lines he has tentatively introduced into the draft. That is, he uses language to refer to its own ground in an obscure process, so that its articulations appear as disconnected, limited, and in opposition; and therefore as emerging. Language itself cannot speak of the mystery of the relation of creature to creation; but this *use* of language can mirror the mystery.

In the fourth stanza the content of the metaphor refers to the relation of creator to creature and the language itself is evidently the creature of the poet. But in the fifth stanza the introduction of image and meaning via language is again such as to render these symbolic, to give them a

reference to their own ground in a process out of which
that articulation which is language emerges. The poet introduces the image of the hosts of heaven, "the stars threw
down their spears," and the image of the creator of that
Lamb whom we know from earlier and other poems to be
Christ; but he does it in such a way that we hover between
images. Indeed, the words and phrases strain and break,
they fail to become precise, and we sense their articulating
movement as decaying, so that they fall back into the
process from which they sprang. Thus we are told the
hosts of heaven threw down their spears, and we seek to
fix this image. Was it because of the nature of the tiger?
Did they refuse to celebrate creation and disavow the
leadership of such a creator? Perhaps, for they watered
heaven with their tears. Yet Blake suggests that the creator
smiled at his own work, whatever the heavenly hosts may
have thought. Or, since Blake asks if the creator smiled,
perhaps the thought is that he did not. We have very little
evidence for answering the question of the last line of the
stanza one way or the other. "Did he who made the Lamb
make thee?" We do not know! The variety, the opposition
of the words and images introduced are such as prevent
full articulation, so that these creatures of the poet give
evidence that the poet is not the creator of clear and definite results, participant in creation though he is.

The last stanza affirms this insight. At the level of the
content of the images and phrases we return to the tiger
and the fire, for the last stanza repeats the first with the
exception of one word. We return to the tiger having ex-
plored the idea of the creature as a product of a creator,
somehow like man, with negative results, so that now we

accept the tiger and the fire in the relationship of creature to creation. We accept the question in the last two lines, "What immortal hand or eye dare frame thy fearful symmetry?," as rhetorical, as having a negative answer. But if we are willing now to view the articulation of the creature as having little similarity to the process of fabrication by a human creator, however extrapolated, it is because the poet has shown us how the articulation of image and meaning can refer, not to the poet as creator, but through the poet as contributor back to the movement of the art-work which leads into an aesthetic occasion. When the poet comes to stand in this position by introducing image and meaning in such a way as to permit their multiplication and the generation of ambiguity, articulation becomes a sustaining aspect of disclosing content. Thus the humanity of the poet, his need for explicitness of image and meaning, is transmuted into participation in an aesthetic occasion; the poet stands, not as maker, but as one who offers his nature as a sustainer of this occasion.

In other art forms, too, in music, in painting, in prose, for example, the human meaning which the medium carries or can be made to carry may be transformed into symbol. When such a transformation is achieved by the artist, the activities of forming which disclose content are characterized as articulation. In any medium the significance of a symbol is that it reveals the disclosure of content as an articulating movement. The effect of this revelation is to accord to the aesthetic occasion a continuation. The transformation of meaning into symbols suggests multiple meanings emerging out of the movement in the art-work leading into an aesthetic occasion. The suggested meanings appear as an efflorescence of the movement disclosing content, as a development of this movement which reveals its nature. Its nature is to be found not in the meanings which are suggested, but in the movement toward them; a movement which—as developing toward these meanings in disclosing content—testifies to the accessibility of this disclosure to man, and to the effectiveness of man's participation in the disclosure. Participation in an aesthetic occasion is not only accident; those activities leading into it are not entered upon merely by chance —this becomes clear when they are seen as an expression of human nature in their efflorescence into a myriad of meanings. At the same time it becomes clear that the human nature thus expressed has a different orientation than that expressed in the images and meanings as such. It is by taking this orientation, by transmuting his nature, that the artist is able to enter into the art-work and to contribute to it, to participate in an aesthetic occasion and to sustain it. The *presence* of an aesthetic occasion is evidence that man is bringing it forward.

IV. *Patterns of Creation: Art-Forms and Renewal*

We say we are going to a play, or to hear a concert. We read poetry. We visit a museum in order to see paintings. We study modern architecture, or examine Greek sculpture. Even more particularly, we are in the audience of a one-act play, or we read a short story. We prefer lyrics, we observe, to ballads or to dramatic poetry. In the museum we neglect the oils for the water colors, or perhaps for the prints. Our delight may be in genre sculpture, or in contemporary welded-metal abstractions; or we may find medieval cathedrals essentially more interesting than Greek temples or modern business buildings. And, of course, we may listen to a string quartet, a woodwind quintet, a classical symphony, or some other of the many forms of musical composition. As connoisseurs of Chinese painting we may knowingly distinguish between the styles prevalent in the Ch'ing dynasty—the varieties of art are very many indeed.

When we approach art from ordinary experience, the variety of distinguishable art-forms seems patent. As in other areas of human existence, our need to deal with variety leads us to categorize and define. Perhaps the easiest, if least satisfactory, conception of art-forms is based upon some principle of similarity of art-objects. The whole of Chinese painting is usually presented chronologically in terms of the Chinese dynasties and the periods which comprise them. The fact that paintings were created in the same political era is useful for mnemonic purposes: it permits books to be organized, and it enables courses to be taught. It permits the writing of a history of Chinese painting. Even broader organization based upon occurrence together in time and space is common. We have a history of oriental art, of Greek art, of primitive art. And, for one purpose or another, such a history is to the point. But valuable as any history of art-objects may be, it seems to have little to do with art, that is, with art-works. Evidently the patterns of similarity which make such a history possible are external to the art-work.

Another common approach to defining art-forms, which seems more relevant to the art-work, is based upon observation not of the chance occurrence of art-objects together in an area of space or a period of time, but of the broad differences between art-objects having a spatial structure and those having a temporal pattern. One may say that music, dance, and poetry develop in successive moments, while painting, sculpture, and architecture are statically structured. Evident as this is of the art-objects in question, it is clearly false of the art-works which develop out of creative activities and appreciative responses related to these objects. This may be illustrated by the case of the appreciator of architecture. Response to architecture is response to a building having a spatial configuration; but it involves an activity which takes place through successive moments. This we see by observing an appreciator of the cathedral at Chartres approaching it across the plain of Beauce, examining its varied aspects, wandering through its interior; and if we happen to be the appreciator, we know, too, that this external process reflects a movement leading into an aesthetic occasion. Granting the centrality of the art-work, a division of the arts on the basis of space and time seems arbitrary. Is there then a basis for conceiving of art-forms as more closely related to creative action and appreciative response?

Perhaps a conception of art-forms as related to the different modes of human perception would have this character. Such a view, when offered, usually takes the form of distinguishing between the arts in terms of the media used in them. Quite evidently each material of art has its own nature, with its own possibilities and limitations. Different materials seem to have irreducibly different aesthetic effects. Thus stone and pigments and tones are not the same and make a different contribution to art. It seems easy to catch this difference of contribution and to define an art-form and relate it to the art-work, on the basis of different human perceptual capacities used in responding to the different media. For example, we may note that music appeals to the sense of hearing, whereas painting appeals to the sense of sight. Evidently, music is built up from tones, each having a rather precise pitch, and arranged in intervals on a scale; that is to say, the materials of music are available to man's sense of hearing. Further, the use of varied instruments and their part in a composition results in audible differences, thus opening the way to distinctions within the general category of music. The compass of the instruments used in music, their ability to accent and articulate, and the strength and survival quality of their tones are readily detectable and allow for the determination of a variety of musical species. By contrast painting uses media which appeal to the eye. The painter works with pigments, with line and shape, and with pattern.

This plausible difference between painting and music as art-forms tends to vanish when we focus our attention more sharply upon the nature of response to the media. Response, in the case of the artist, can hardly be channeled in one sense. The artist is attracted to media to which he is especially sensitive perceptually; but his response to such a medium is by no means limited to perception. The artist responds to his medium through his whole personality, which, brought to a focus in his creative imagination, serves to guide and control his manipulation of the medium. The creative imagination involves experience and memory as well as the artist's range of values, and the manipulation of a medium is in part a physical process of modification and control. The artist's response to his medium is not merely perceptual; it is a spiritual action, but a physical one as well; it is an act involving causal agency, but also guided by a heightened sense of possibility.

In the case of the appreciator aesthetic response is not limited to, or even dominated by, a single sense. The tones of which music is built carry rhythms, and if our appreciation of these rhythms is initiated aurally, our full involvement with them depends upon a broad response of our body and nervous system, not to mention our past experience, our personality, and our imaginative talents. The rhythms developed by percussion instruments are felt as much as heard. There are rhythms in a painting which no doubt reach us through the eye, but to which we respond, in virtue of kinaesthesis, with the musculature and nerves of our body, and through our body with our mind and spirit. If we ask whether poetry appeals to the eye or ear, our answer must be both and more. Ballads and epics were (and are) directed to the ear. Historically, the means of their communication has been recitation and declamation. Yet there are many poems which are intended to be read silently, and which appeal to the eye not only in being written down, but by means of visual devices such as arrangement of lines, use of capitals, and punctuation. Read aloud or silently, an art-work developed from a poem involves rhythms, imagery, and values, which are neither seen directly nor heard, and which presuppose a response by the body, personality, and mind of the appreciator.

The integral relation of creative or appreciative response to the art-work clearly rules out a definition of an art-form solely in the terms of art-objects or the media of art; but it does suggest that an adequate conception of an art-form might be framed in the terms of such response. One way of following out this suggestion has been to consider the creative or appreciative handling of the media of the arts in terms of the modes of expression which characterize this handling. On this view the handling of media essential to the development of an art-work is characterized by the expression of a dominant value or cluster of values. We may conceive of architecture as an art-form because the development of an architectural art-work is colored by the expression of values to be found in man's relation to society. The handling of those materials of which buildings are made, the earth, stone, bricks, wood, iron, and glass, typically conveys the sense of their permanence and endurance into an expression of those more enduring and stable patterns of human society. Thus in the building of or dwelling in a house we find expressed the immemorial unity of the family. We may expect to appreciate in a capitol the majesty of a politically organized community; and in a monument the commemoration of the sacrifice or service of the individual to the group. Similarly, we may conceive of literature as an art-form because the development of a literary art-work is definitively marked by the expression of meaning. The handling of words typically conveys the sense of the significance and value of meaning. In a novel we find expressed the range of meaning extending from the immediate to the discursive; a lyric poem expresses the value of imagery and sharp emotion.

The determination of the nature of an art-form by fixing its characteristic kind of expression is beset with difficulties precisely because the art-object also has a part to play. There are buildings which exact a response, not of social values, but of individual whim; personal monuments and purely ornamental structures do likewise. There is literature which is no more characterized by meaning than painting. The truth is that the idea of an art-form is a complex concept and although it involves reference to art-objects, to media and modes of perception, and to expression, an adequate formulation of this concept is not possible in the terms of any one of these elements. As the preceding account indicates, an attempt to fix the significance of the art-form in terms of one of these elements leads to ambiguity when another element is taken into consideration. The same medium may be handled to give different expressions, and the same expression may be found in response to widely different art-objects. Yet the idea of an art-form is not completely relative. What is universal in it is best approached through a consideration of the contributions made to the art-work by the creative activities of the artist which have reference to all the factors we have considered.

When we consider the creative activities of an artist, we envision him as selecting a medium to which he is especially sensitive, of handling this medium in terms of the techniques he has learned and perfected, of enriching his manipulation of materials by allowing the personality he has acquired and developed to influence his actions, of reflecting in these actions more or less of the temper and tone of his culture, and of bringing these diverse strands into relation in the creative fusion of an imaginative synthesis which is controlled to some extent by the artist's conscious intention. Many aspects of such creative activities have been mentioned and discussed in the preceding pages in relation to other issues and in order to cast light upon other facets of art. What has not yet been done is to discuss these activities in their own right, that is, as activities which relate to a medium, which develop expression and result in an art-object while reflecting the contribution which the artist makes to the art-work in the interests of an aesthetic occasion. It is the explicit reflection of this contribution which is the central strand in the conception of the art-form.

An explicit reflection of this contribution may be seen in the fact that artists inaugurate new movements in art. In doing this they relate their own creative participation in art-works to the history and tradition of art. Artists turn from instances of art-objects which result from common modes of creative forming and try to provide modifications of these modes and, so, a different kind of art-object. Artists see their own forming activities as reflecting a long tradition of artistic achievement, the origins of which are lost in time, and the renewal of which is to be the fruit of their efforts. That is, artists see themselves as accepting the necessity to break with tradition in order to move more adequately through the art-work into an aesthetic occasion, and as having the courage to make this break. This more adequate movement into the aesthetic occasion comes to be grasped as a human contribution made through the modification of modes of creative forming. But what exactly is contributed? In what does this greater adequacy result? We have noted that when extra-aesthetic values are introduced into art in contrast to aesthetic elements, the inception of an aesthetic occasion may occur; and that when meanings are developed into symbols in the art-work this may evoke the presence of an aesthetic occasion. We ask now what a renewal of the artistic enterprise introduces into the aesthetic occasion.

When attained through a renewal of the artistic enterprise, through a kind of revolution of art, the aesthetic occasion mirrors the sweep of a history in which, from an unknown beginning toward an unknown end, man offers his powers for art. The artist who formulates this answer outside of his art—that is, by stating the nature of a program—often does so by insisting upon renewing the significance of art for man; something he proposes to do by a reconception of creative forming activity. Thus Louis Sullivan in *The Autobiography of an Idea* proposes that the principle of the new architecture is to be that "form follows function." He intends that line, plane, and space be brought into relation to the human purposes of a building: its use as a home, as a school, as a church. The explicit suggestion in Sullivan's words, if not the implicit suggestion of his buildings, is that architecture serves man's already existing purposes. It is fairly evident from what he says, however, that this function is not to be understood externally, but that the result of the new architecture will be a change in man and in human life, that is, in man's purposes. Frank Lloyd Wright formulated his program in a way which makes this clearer. He urged that the "classical" architecture with its static forms be replaced by an architecture in which space is central, and in which there is flow instead of stasis:

Classic architecture was all fixation . . . now . . . let walls, ceilings, floors become seen as component parts of each other, their surfaces flowing into each other's . . . Have no posts, no columns . . . In my work the idea of plasticity may be seen as the element of continuity . . . the new reality that is space instead of matter.

But what is the significance of this new reality which has been achieved through the redefinition of creative forming activity? Wright said:

Architecture, I believed, was bound to become more humanely significant . . . Architecture of the machine-age should become not only fundamental to our culture but natural to the happiness of our lives as well . . . All building should serve the liberation of mankind, liberating the lives of individuals.

The new architecture is not merely to serve man, but to free him. The new architecture is to transmute man, to be an architecture of democracy, of which, Wright added, Whitman was the prophet.

The verbal abstractions of this program were embodied in the creative enterprise as it was modified to reflect the program. Architects turned to new media, choosing paper, glass, aluminum, and concrete. They modified their techniques to deal with these media and to manipulate the old media in different ways for different ends. They developed new techniques, as for the use of glass and the pouring of concrete. They oriented their personalities toward and guided their creative imagination by the new vision. They demanded a change in the temper and social patterns of the times in order to adapt them to the new architecture.

In all this demand for change and the introduction of novelty they underlined the contribution made by creative activity in the development of an art-work, insisting upon its place. In the kind of change they demanded and the variety of novelty they introduced, they made quite clear the fact that contribution to an art-work requires something of man, and their architecture reflects this quest for the man who can contribute, the men who can dwell in their buildings. Such a modification of creative activities reveals the contributor to an art-work as a participator, reveals, that is, a movement through the art-work toward incorporation of the artist, and in turn the appreciator, in the aesthetic occasion. In the new architecture this is reflected in the sense one often has of the development of continuous, flowing space to become a cradle for man, a place of his rebirth. Thus the disclosing of content in such architecture is characterized by a movement incorporating man, a movement which is a continuous development toward man as artist. At the end of Chapter Two we called a continuing disclosure of content a realm. We now may see that a realm involves not only a continuous disclosure, but a movement incorporating man as renewing and continuing this disclosure.

The new architecture is not the only architecture which has the power to evoke a realm. Indeed, the medieval cathedral often has this power. And any art-form, conceived along the lines sketched for the new architecture, may evoke a realm. The modification of existing patterns of creative activities in such a way as to aid in the development of an art-work renews the human significance of art. It is this modification and renewal which we call the *art-*

form. It is this modification and renewal which makes explicit the contribution of the artist (and in his own way, that of the appreciator) to the art-work, a contribution which at once renews and continues the disclosure of content and reflects the transmuted nature of man as participant in renewed disclosure.

V. *Man's Place in Art*

Faust, in Thomas Mann's version, is presented as striving to encompass everything human in the forms of art, specifically in the strict forms of music, thereby hoping to gain control of man and his nature. Mann suggests that the result of such an effort is madness, and Faust is depicted as insane as, or just before, he achieves his goal. Human passion for participation in art is presented here with emphasis upon the character of art as dissociated from general human culture. Presented also, is the seductive character of art, its danger to things human; the fact that the man who is preoccupied with aesthetic experience and with art is not quite human in any ordinary sense.

It is true that art has a strange and a dangerous quality. Yet this strangeness and danger lie not so much in the estrangement of art from things human, as in the change which things human, and human nature, undergo when they are incorporated into art. The discussion of reflexive forms in this Chapter has been intended to give an account of this incorporation, an account which comes to one focus in the suggestion that human nature is modified to be incorporated in art when it burns in the creative fire.

There is an evident sense in which an artist is a contributor and an analogous though weaker sense in which appreciative response is contributive to art. The artist devotes himself to his aesthetic task, he selects and handles his media in order to sustain and develop this orientation, he modifies the traditional patterns of his predecessors in order to attain a distinctive style of his own. Such activities, whether sketched in this cursory way, or discussed in detail, are contributory to art. When an artist, or in his own way an appreciator, engages in such activities there is an intention to contribute in some fashion to the art-work. That such intentions are not always fulfilled, we know from the eloquent accounts of artists noting the rising and falling of their creative powers, and from our own experience as appreciators which varies from extreme sensitivity at one time to definite opaqueness at another. The activities in which an artist engages may fail to develop an art-work, and the art-object he produces may fail to serve a subsequent appreciator in his entering the art-work. When the development of an art-work cannot be managed, the difficulty is often due to the inhibition of aesthetic response by ordinary human activities; activities which obscure the path into the art-work with the shadow of man's extra-aesthetic interests, his preoccupation with meanings, and even his learned artistic responses. The selection of a medium and its forming may be so definitely controlled by the conscious human interests and goals of the artist, for example, as to preclude that receptivity, dual to contribution, which provides access to an art-work.

Contribution to an art-work is effective in leading into an aesthetic occasion when it is action which also receives —the contributor must be a participator. The orienta-

tion of the artist toward the art-work becomes a true contribution when it results in participation. This can happen
when such orientation involves openness, when modes of
handling and control of development of media introduce
meanings, as the personality of the artist and the temper
of the times, as open to the given. Extra-aesthetic values
can be introduced into the art-work not in their own right,
but used in contrast or in functional design to call attention to the art-object and, so, lead through this into the
aesthetic occasion. The introduction of meanings may be
accomplished in such a way as to use their existence
(rather than their significance) as evidence of the articulating movement in the disclosure of content. Such *use* of
extra-aesthetic value and meaning deprecates the explicit
significance of value and meaning and focuses attention
upon them as aspects of the art-work. Their *use* by the
artist (or appreciator) gives to them a double reference:
they still carry something of the explicit significance which
any value or meaning has, but they carry this significance,
in virtue of their *use*, on the basis of their occurrence in the
art-work. Thus the *use* of value and meaning in the context of art sets a boundary to these, defines the limit of
their significance, and reveals them in relation to what is
not intrinsically valuable or meaningful. The artistic activities in such *use* produce an awareness of the boundary of
human significance, reveal what is peculiarly human as
limited and finite, by showing its relation to what is other
than man.

The receptivity requisite to participation in an aesthetic
occasion is found only when the contributive activities of
the artist express human finitude in the midst of the de-

velopment of the art-work. This can occur only when the boundaries of human value and meaning are made explicit in relation to the given. When this condition is fulfilled, contribution to an art-work becomes action which evokes and sustains the disclosure of content, becomes, that is, creative action in and through which the artist participates in the art-work. This creative action, characterized by participation, is itself intended by the artist. To this end, the artist modifies the traditional patterns of creative action. He introduces art-forms in order to become a participator.

The goal of the artist is to become creative; his end in view is to participate in an aesthetic occasion. This end may be conceived too easily as a goal for which it is necessary to find the means. From the point of view of one who wishes to participate in an aesthetic occasion, the activities of forming may seem to be the means to be used to achieve the nature of a participator; but such an external perspective is fundamentally misleading. The movement of creative activity, thus, is not that of orientation toward an aesthetic occasion and development thereof; it is not a movement directed from a beginning toward a goal of participation by man become artist to achieve this end. The participator is to be found only in participation, and there only in and through forming activities when these are creative. Participation, then, is a movement having an inception which reflects its creative element, but a movement which expresses its creative element not as directed toward an end, but as the presence of the aesthetic occasion, as an enlarging of intuition. That this presence is not directed, is more clearly understood when its creative element is grasped as renewal, as introducing an inception which repeats and defines.

The idea of man transmuted to become artist, of man as creative, as participator, is not introduced into the art-work via the art-form to provide a transcendent goal for which contributive activities are means. Quite the contrary, this idea is introduced to express, first, the fact that contributive activity is qualified by the limitedness, the boundedness of those values and meanings which characterize the humanity of the contributor; and that, in consequence of this bound, such forming depends upon what is other than the contributor. But, second, this idea is introduced to express the fact that what is other than the contributor must be taken up in creative action if this is to lead into disclosure of content. This acceptance of what is other than the contributor takes place in the context of the art-form. It occurs through the modification of creative patterns which presupposes that in the past what is other than man has been accepted, and which moves on to new modes of creation which can accept what has now been revealed as beyond human bounds. The idea of creativity refers to the participator as the renewer and continuer of the disclosure of content. The renewal in the aesthetic occasion found in the context of the art-form presupposes not only a contributive forming activity, but the participation of the artist in a process which has other contributors than him, other contributions to which he is receptive in his creative role. Participation in the realm of art by man demands and needs what is other than man, something which man transmuted to become artist can accept and to which he can respond.

CHAPTER 4

TRANSCENDENTAL FORM: COMEDY

I. Negative Elements

There is a poem by Bertolt Brecht called "The Mask of Evil" which reads,

> An meiner Wand hängt ein japanisches Holzwerk
> Maske eines bösen Dämons, bemalt mit Goldlack.
> Mitfühlend sehe ich
> Die geschwollenen Stirnadern, andeutend
> Wie anstrengend es ist, böse zu sein.*

What a strain it is to be evil? In art, perhaps; where form tends to dominate and overcome elements of evil when they are introduced. For, as we have observed in the course of Chapter Two, the forms of art reveal content which emerges in this forming. An aesthetic occasion of this sort defines the beginnings of art, and such an occasion is never subject-matter. This much is clear. Yet is the demon who is the subject of the mask transformed by the lines, the figures and planes, by the color and texture into an aesthetic occasion which is no longer evil? To some extent the forming which characterizes the mask as artwork does dominate the demon; yet not completely, perhaps. The threat of the demon may still be felt behind these patterns of the wooden mask.

And yet is this threat any more than man's sense of forces inimical to him expressed in the symbol of a demon?

* On my wall hangs a Japanese carving,
  The mask of an evil demon, decorated with gold lacquer.
  Sympathetically I observe
  The swollen veins of the forehead, indicating
  What a strain it is to be evil.

95

Is not the significance of evil for human hopes caught in the image of the demon and so transformed by reflexive forming into an aspect of the aesthetic occasion? And does not this mean that evil has been changed into something human? And is this not all that evil can be? Could there be any elements in art which are not caught in the elementary forming activities found, for example, in line, figure, and symmetry, and also not caught by the reflexive forming activities we have just discussed in Chapter Three and which elicit inception, presence, and renewal? Are there elements in art which might be called negative elements?

Let us consider another example from Brecht in which evil is presented most starkly, so starkly that it seems hardly to be caught in reflexive forms, hardly to have any human meaning at all which might be used in reflexive forms. In his poem entitled "Great Thanksgiving Chorus" Brecht begins each stanza with a peculiarly forceful line, as follows:

Lobet die Nacht and die Finsternis, die euch umfangen!

Lobet das Gras und die Tiere, die neben euch leben und sterben!

Lobet den Baum, der aus Aas aufwächst jauchzend zum Himmel!

Lobet von Hertzen das schlechte Gedächtnis des Himmels!

Lobet die Kälte, die Finsternis und das Verderben! *

* Praise ye the night and the darkness which surround you!

96

But what is this night and darkness, this unmindfulness of heaven, this cold, and this carrion and corruption?

What are these elements? Clearly, they are not merely evils which as threatening to man may be symbolized as demons and so serve to form the art-work reflexively. The poet presents these elements as ultimate evils, as elements a part of whose force cannot be given a human significance at all, and so as elements which can be dealt with only by the kind of recognition of their strangeness which is found in the praise of thanksgiving. Of course these elements do have some human significance; but here they are not presented in and through such terms. Quite the contrary, they are presented in such a way as to diminish their human significance, and their impact and place in the poem depends upon this. In consequence, they, and other similar elements, deserve especial attention. We shall call such elements *negative elements* because they are used by the artist in a way which opposes them to meanings of other expressive elements to be found in art.

No doubt any element in an art-work has human meaning and significance. At the very least it was introduced into the art-work by the artist (or an appreciator) and carries his stamp; yet the intention of the artist need not be to make use of its human significance for the disclosure

---

Praise ye the grass and the beast which neighbor you, living and dying!

. . . .

Praise ye the tree which groweth exultant from carrion unto heaven!

. . . .

Praise ye from your hearts the unmindfulness of heaven!

. . . .

Praise ye the cold, the darkness and corruption!

of content. Indeed, the artist may intend to make use of elements in disclosing content just by ignoring whatever positive human significance they may have acquired. This occurs, for one example, in Melville's *Typee*. This is a story of life in the South Seas, and life there is presented as an idyll. It is Melville himself, who, having deserted a whaler, is caught up by the bounty of life and in the freedom of existence on those southern islands. There, the grace and beauty attending natural expression are the rule, something Melville seeks to depict in many ways, and which in his hands becomes the symbol of what is of human value. Thus, he describes a boating excursion with Fayaway in lines which carry this humanly positive aspect of the story:

> With a wild exclamation of delight, [Fayaway] disengaged from her person the ample robe of tappa which was knotted over her shoulder (for the purpose of shielding her from the sun), and spreading it out like a sail, stood erect with upraised arms in the head of the canoe. We American sailors pride ourselves upon our straight clean spars, but a prettier little mast than Fayaway made was never shipped aboard of any craft.

Yet, having detailed an idyll, Melville introduces into his account the altar behind the native village and the cannibalistic rites performed there. This is surely deliberate on his part, and one must suppose that he conceives the presentation of this evil to serve an artistic purpose. Of course one may seem to grasp this purpose in the terms of human value which can serve the ends of reflexive forming. That is, one may say that the detail of the altar rounds out the picture of life in the South Seas, giving the whole story. The satisfying sense of completeness so engendered not only pulls the reader further into the story and so enhances the development of the art-work; but it is reflected directly in and augments the aesthetic unity of formed-content which is an aspect of inception and presence. Or, again, one may see the function of the account of the altar as of direct significance for reflexive forming. That is, one may see this detail as a contrasting meaning, in opposition to the idyll, and so as introducing the ambiguity of meanings which is so necessary in order to evoke the presence of formed-content. There is nothing wrong with this kind of explanation of the presentation of evil. Such explanations are correct, so far as they go; but such explanations hardly seem to give a sufficient account of Melville's artistic intentions. The sharpness of the contrast between the good natural life and the practice of cannibalism as he presents it is too great. He does nothing to modify this sharpness; he leaves it as stark as he can in order, apparently, to accomplish an aesthetic purpose which a negative element alone can fulfill.

Melville's intention here, in his employment of evil, is quite different from other cases where evil is a part of the expressive aspects of a story, and so occurs as such only by accident. We find many instances of this latter use in *Grimms' Fairy Tales*. Many of these tales contain episodes which seem cruel and which even involve evil; and we might suppose that they were intentionally introduced to achieve some special aesthetic purpose. Probably this is not so. When we are told of the sufferings of animals and the beating of children, for example, such occurrences seem to be parts, merely, or descriptive accounts; that is,

99

to be a part of the representative aspect of the story. As such they have no special significance because of their apparent emphasis upon cruelty.

Such lines as:

The poor little nestlings lay on the ground, fluttering and flapping their wings and crying: "We poor helpless children must feed ourselves, and we can't even fly! We shall die of hunger. There is nothing else for it."

The good youth dismounted, killed his horse with his sword, and left the carcass as food for the young ravens. They hopped up to it and cried, "We will remember and reward you."

probably did not seem particularly cruel to those who told and retold these tales, or to those who first listened to them. There has been some development of human sensitivity to cruelty over the past few centuries; and details which strike us today with great force would probably go unremarked by earlier audiences. More fundamentally, we may observe that in these tales the excessive cruelty serves no recognizable artistic purpose.

Yet there are instances of art, like Melville's *Typee* and, even more, his later works, where the introduction of evil is clearly deliberate; where, in fact, the function of evil is so central to the artistic enterprise as to be necessary for a statement of the theme of the piece.

Another instance in which there is a clear use of negative elements which fall outside the realm of human meaning and which fulfill their function just for this reason, is the Hindu myth of Markandeya. This myth deals with some singular adventures of a very old and incredibly wise man. So wise has he grown in the course of his long and saintly life that it is difficult to suppose that he has anything more to learn about virtue or religion. And this is the point of the tale; that human life and meaning has nothing more to teach him, that the ultimate mysteries transcend this realm. To make this point elements are introduced into the tale which refer to the unknown and strange in such a way as to incorporate these into the story.

The myth begins with the traditional Hindu account of the deterioration of the universe from the golden age, the age of full virtue. The course of this change is depicted as passing through the successively deteriorating ages of man's civilization, including the present, until having reached the age which epitomizes evil and lawlessness, in which occurs the ultimate in egotism and vice, this most degenerate age is devoured by fire and the dust of the holocaust is laid by a torrential rain which gradually collects to form the ocean of non-being, the night of Brahma. In this night of non-being, the great god Vishnu sleeps; all has become and remains implicit. And yet the ocean of non-being is filled with the waters of life, so that even as Vishnu floats sleeping upon the ocean he dreams. And in the dream of the god, the sage, Markandeya, lives a life of perfect holiness. Yet while living this dreamed life, the sage inadvertently slips from the mouth of Vishnu and falls into the waters of non-being. In consequence he finds himself swimming desperately in the dark waters and finds his situation unbelievable; indeed, he supposes that this might be a dream, for the strangeness of the situation is totally beyond his human powers of comprehension. But before the sage can adjust to this situation in any way, Vishnu stirs in his sleep and, scooping him up out of the water, returns him to the dream. This one excursion into absolute strangeness is followed, in the tale, by two more. In the next Markandeya again slips from the dream of the god into the waters of non-existence—but sees floating upon them the great figure of the sleeping god. And, finally, when he slips into the waters for the third time, he sees upon them an island where the great and venerable god Vishnu is seated and playing as a child. In the myth Markandeya is pictured as being returned, at last, to the dream of perfect existence, never having grasped the awful significance of his adventure.

Although there are many expressive elements in this story, its theme and one aspect of its form must be sought elsewhere than in these. Evidently the theme of the tale is developed through the introduction of the uncanny into it, that is, the uncanny appears in the tale as what is unknown and unknowable to man. This myth differs from many in religion in not trying to render the ultimate mysteries comprehensible to man. The uncanny is deliberately introduced into the story and it is clear that a great deal of artistry has gone into the handling of this element. Our present task is to try to understand the nature of this introduction and the effect it has in an aesthetic occasion.

Let us begin with a fundamental similarity between the introduction and handling of negative elements and expressive elements in an art-work. The artistry in both cases is directed to revealing explicitly that the aesthetic process in which content is disclosed is sustained by sources which are partly external to it. It is evident that the introduction of expressive elements places man in art; but it is evident, too, that the handling of these elements makes explicit the complexity of this relation of man to art. How does man have a place in art? We have indicated that this place is that of creative activity, which, in part, involves the exercise of technical skills of a high order on the media the artist selects. Still, William Blake was right when he insisted that skill could not promote progress in art, for "To suppose that art can go beyond the finest specimens of art that are now in the world is not knowing what art is: it is being blind to the gifts of the Spirit." The place of a creator in art is not that of one who has sufficient power to produce art, but, rather, of one who through an alteration of his own nature makes a contribution to art. Human meanings and values, when introduced by the creative artist, are made to stand in relation to the dynamic process of the art-work. In this relation their significance is not to be found in meaning and value as such, but in their help in sustaining, in continuing the aesthetic occasion which emerges in the art-work; something revealed in the inception, presence, and renewal of this occasion when the artist comes to stand in relation to it as explicitly creative. The use of expressive elements introduces man into art; but this introduction involves demands upon man, demands which he cannot meet in the terms of the nature which he brings to art. For man to be a source of art, a contributor to it, he must become creative. Thus the use of expressive elements in art introduces a quest for man as creative, and art in which expressive elements are properly handled itself formulates a question concerning man's nature as creative.

In a similar way, the introduction of negative elements is intended to place what is other than man explicitly into art, and to reveal something of the part this plays and the nature it comes to have in the art-work. These elements raise a question concerning the nature of what is other than man as participant in an aesthetic occasion.

What is negative about a negative element in art? Certainly not its significance for the art-work. The qualification "negative" means only that the element in question gains its significance from its presentation as outside the realm of human meanings, from its reference to a source of the art-work which is other than man. In art the elements of ugliness, pain, and the tragic most evidently fall into the category of negative elements, for these most obviously stand opposed to the realm of positive human values. There are other elements in art which must be included in this category as well. These are the elements which are introduced to give the patterns of the comic across all its many variations; for the comic transcends the realm of human meanings as much as the tragic, if not so apparently.

When we speak of man, whether as artist or as appreciator, as a source of an art-work we refer to the contribution to art in virtue of his nature *and* to the modification of his nature required for participation in an aesthetic occasion. By analogy, when we speak of a non-human source of an art-work, we need to refer to a similar contribution *and* modification. But while it is relatively easy to take account of man's contribution to an art-work by referring to human skills and expressive elements as serving a function there, it is not so easy to take account of the non-human contribution. By what name can we speak of it? That is, how can we treat it without inadvertently making it into something human?

Perhaps the best name, and one that explicitly contains the reference to the non-human, is to call it the *other*. This is a very opaque term, of necessity; and it will be necessary to use more revealing ones on occasion, as has been done already in referring to evil as an element in art. To refer to the other in the context of a discussion of an art-work is, after all, not merely to refer to a non-human source of an art-work; there is reference as well to the modification of this source through its participation in an aesthetic occasion. From the perspective of a human participant in disclosing content, the other is not only given; but, as itself a participant in disclosing content, it is a giving. The other constitutes what is given, but it is also taken up into and changed in the art-work, and, so, it accords something to the content disclosed in this process.

To speak of man as a source of the art-work, and to conceive of him as a contributor engaged in elementary forming activities, carries directly to a sense of the transmutation of man's nature through his contribution; for our sense of our own active participation in an aesthetic occasion involves a sense of giving and transmutation of ourselves through this giving. The materials of art are given relative to the art-work, and as materials they constitute a basis for distinction within it. The materials of art are a basis for color, texture, or tone, for example; and we are aware of such distinctions as arising from this non-human source. We not only have a sense of materials yielding to the requirements of the art-work, but of their according to an aesthetic occasion something of what is there. Yet the awareness of the capacity of materials to be transmuted in an art-work does not carry so directly into a quest for what the other might become through art. The reason for this is simply that a conception of the other is not available to the artist. Reflexive forms show that man's nature is transformed in relation to the art-work to become a being who stands within and sustains an aesthetic occasion. This explicit formulation through reflexive forms is possible because they reflect aspects of human nature which are directly available to the artist.

The explicit formulation of the transformation of the other into that which stands within and sustains an aesthetic occasion can be achieved by the artist only indirectly. The formulation of this transformation, thus, must involve a presentation of man's orientation toward the other; a presentation of man as accepting the other. By this mediate means the artist may form the art-work in such a way as to express the possibility of the other coming to stand in and sustain the aesthetic occasion. He does this, we have said, implicitly through the use of materials, and explicitly by calling upon himself as creator (or the appreciator) or upon a human protagonist in the art-work to accept the contribution to the art-work and participation in an aesthetic occasion by the other. But it is time to consider the means the artist uses to formulate this acceptance.

II. *The Comic and the Comic Form*

In ordinary discussions about art, we tend to speak of a comedy as an art form which is predominantly pleasant, and thus as an art which is not tragic. This usage may lead to a misunderstanding of the nature of the comic form, for it suggests that comedies, as pleasant, are all essentially variants of reflexive forms. Now all comedies abound in pleasurable elements, and it is true that whatever other function these may have, they can serve as expressions of human pleasure and so serve to give expressive form to the art-work in which they appear. In a play, the fanciful and imaginative plot and situations which make it a comedy can be taken as expressive of man's nature and as contributions to reflexive form. The ribald, the enticing, the idyllic, for instance, are expressions of man's nature and they are widely used in comic art. For this very reason the task of distinguishing comic form from reflexive form is both more difficult and more important. Although comedies abound in pleasurable elements, the expressive significance of these serves a secondary function; their primary function is to contribute to a distinct comic form, which is not a reflexive form.

To understand the primary place of the pleasant and its variations in comic form let us begin, not with a sophisticated play or other developed instance, but with the raw material of comedy. Let us begin with the simplest comic situations, that is, with our characteristic response to the naïve. We often laugh at children's actions: their mode of walking, their attempts to enter into social relations, their mimicry of adult activities. If we see a small child walking, the seriousness and intensity of his efforts and the exaggerated and stilted character of his accomplishment make us smile. He moves each foot carefully through a wide arc and places it firmly, meanwhile focusing his whole attention upon his efforts. If he should happen to fall, we may be solicitous of his welfare; but, still, we move to his aid, often as not, laughing. Or, for another example, tension between adolescent girls and boys makes us smile when we see their more or less unsuccessful efforts to resolve it through the channels of social relations. We may be aware of the emotional turmoil and anxiety in the situation, yet the tentative approaches alternating with false assurance, the elaborate ritual invented to give courage, the mistakes and occasional happy successes in this situation are deeply comic. But the paradigm perhaps, of the simple comic situation to which we refer here, is the case of the peasant or provincial in his reactions to the complexity of metropolitan life. Here is one who, wandering through a society with which we are familiar, exhibits at every turn the strangeness of his nature and behavior. He is overawed, inept, gauche, foolish, and ridiculous in his efforts to deal with matters which to us are perfectly ordinary. He comes from another world, really. But, in a sense, all characters in comic situations come from another world.

We see the persons in comic situations such as these as creatures from a different world, creatures whose given nature is such as to prevent them from adequate participation in our world. We laugh at them, at their stumbling inadequacies. We laugh at children who move their lips as they read to themselves, or who stick out their tongues as they write. We laugh at adolescents who strike attitudes of sophistication in their attempts to deal with their new world in which sex is normal. We laugh at the provincial who, gaping at a tall building, falls into a gutter or is robbed by a pickpocket. Yet, seemingly obvious as it is that we do laugh at such people, once we ask *why* we laugh the answer is elusive. Why do we not view these individuals with contempt? Why do we not ignore them as obviously unworthy of notice? They are unable to do what we can do; they have not achieved the abilities and controls which we have won for ourselves.

We are not likely to laugh at these people if more than a certain amount of pain is introduced into the situation in which they find themselves. If the child walking should be injured in a fall we should not laugh; nor should we laugh if the adolescents were driven to suicide, as in *Romeo and Juliet,* by the difficulties of their situation. And, if our sympathies with the provincial are not so easily aroused, still at some point where he is endangered by his naïveté we cease to laugh at him. In any comic situation the point at which we cease to laugh is a variable which is hard to fix. It depends upon the general circumstances, the cultural background we have, and our own characters, for example. Under some circumstances we may laugh at the antics of a baited bear, or at the painful bewilderment of a simple-minded youth at the mercy of insensitive boys. Yet it seems evident that, in principle at least, we laugh at people in a situation only when we respond to the pleasant in the situation; more fundamentally stated, we laugh only when we accept the situation.

Why do we laugh? We laugh at a child because he is dominated by given aspects of his nature which make him a part of the natural situation. We see him as not having achieved the level of humanity which is ours, as dragging his feet of clay. But laughter is always *with* as well as *at*.

We laugh at the child only because we willingly allow the ramparts of our own egos to crumble and accept the patterns of the learning situation and unformed nature which are the child's. Laughter is a response in which we set aside the integrity of our own ego, so hard won, in favor of a natural, a given situation which is indifferent to us and human life as represented by us, and has potentially harmful effects upon our achievements. In this sense our laughter is *with* the child, for we identify with his unformed nature, as contrasted with our achieved character. Comic situations are those in which the natural and given contrast with achieved culture and character; but they are also those in which the natural and given appear as somehow significant and acceptable. In any comic situation, thus, the given must be viewed in such a way as to have an acceptable character.

An easy way to see the given as acceptable is to see it as intrinsically pleasant. To some extent emphasis on the pleasant can be controlled. When we attend a carnival, we orient ourselves in such a way as to pick out what is pleasant and to ignore other elements. In consequence, we laugh over skits in which people take pratfalls, in which esteemed figures are ridiculed, in which characters are beaten, apparently cruelly. Under other circumstances we might laugh at none of these incidents; we are able to laugh because of a more or less unconscious intention to make a selection of experience which emphasizes pleasure. In a similar but much more complicated way, the artist may select the circumstances he depicts in a story or play so as to bring the pleasant to the fore. Thus one of the characteristics common to Mark Twain's *Tom Sawyer,*

Eichendorf's *Aus dem Leben eines Taugenichts,* and Shakespeare's *A Midsummer Night's Dream* is the high pleasure content of the settings, the episodes, and the quality of life of the protagonists. These build an idyll. In them we revel in the delightful. Of course the delights portrayed in these works aid in reflexive forming, they reflect man's place in art. But their primary function as part of a comic situation is not this; rather, it is the presentation of alien circumstances, given situations at which we might laugh, in a way which makes them acceptable to us and, as such, situations evoking laughter. The pleasurable elements which the artist introduces and emphasizes enable us to respond positively to a situation in which the protagonists are revealed as dominated by naïve behavior patterns, natural emotions, and uncontrollable circumstances. If the protagonists fail to control their fate, fail to establish and maintain their egos at a level we would expect, this failure is not one which repulses us. We can accept the failure and the situation occasioning it, because, in part, the situation is presented as so pleasant.

When we say, as we do, that comedy is light and pleasant, we refer, most fundamentally, not to its expressive character, but to an aspect of comic form; that is, to its presentation of a given situation as acceptable, even though its acceptance implies the loss of those achievements which constitute our normal ego and personality. That this is an aspect of comic form may be seen more clearly in somewhat more complex examples of the comic, as caricature and parody. What is least evident in the naïve comic situation of which we have been speaking, is the explicit breaking down of the ramparts of the achieved human personality. In caricature, on the contrary, this is a central and evident point of the artist's intentions. It is even more central in the case of parody. We may see something of this difference by means of examples. Suppose that a small child mimics a rather pompous old professor, but does so simply in the way all small children mimic adults, that is, as a part of his learning processes. Then there is no caricature on the part of the child, although *we* who see the mimicry may take it as caricature. We can function as artists and relate the child's actions to the actions of the old professor in such a way as to see revealed by the child the aging, stilted patterns in the professor's acquired traits. The child's behavior then suggests to us certain behavior of the old man which we otherwise would not notice. In this case *we* caricature. But suppose that a boy of ten years mimics the old professor. In this case the chances are that his intent is malicious, that he wants to reveal the pomposity, the empty knowledge, of the old man. Here the boy is the artist, and he deflates the tacit claims of the old man by parody.

In caricature, the artist emphasizes certain aspects of a person's behavior, attitude, figure, or physiognomy. These traits are true in themselves, but they pass unnoticed until they are selected to reveal the primitive character of the person and so to show him as not what his public personality claims, but as he is elementally. The lines of his nose may suggest a certain crudity of character, a crudeness we have not noticed heretofore because it was concealed by manners and culture. But the artist draws these lines and the man stands revealed to us as quite different from his public image, as a man with a nose of clay. The element of contrast between the public image and the natural man defines a caricature, as such. In fact, of course, most caricatures verge on parody. That is, they include not only the revelation of the natural man, but suggest the destruction of the acquired ego as well. In a parody this destruction is carried out by representing the claims of the ego as nothing but the natural man in disguise. Thus the boy who mimics the old professor may restate the judicious wisdom of the professor as nothing but ignorant temporizing, or he may restate the serious bearing of the professor as nothing but a sense of vain self-importance. The paintings of Jack Levine are parodies in this sense. The *Feast of Pure Reason,* for example, reduces the deliberations of a judge, a banker, and a business man to greed, vanity, and lust. A parody unmasks the elemental man by removing the protective cloak of his developed personality; it does this by revealing the primitive materials out of which this personality has been built by reducing the acquired personality once again to this basis.

In the case of both caricature and parody artistry is required. It may be the artistry of an amateur, that is, of ourselves, as we selectively observe the elements which could go into a sketchy art-work and so serve to caricature or to parody. Or, it may be the artistry of a highly gifted artist who draws, paints, or writes a play. In either case the function of the artistry is similar to the function of pleasurable elements in the case of the naive comic: it serves to render the effect on the personality caricatured or parodied unobjectionable. Caricature and more especially parody have destructive effects, effects which must seem to threaten the persons treated in this way, and especially those with whom

we sympathize. If we were forced to accept without qualification the destruction of personality which is implicit in
a caricature and explicit in parody, we might manage this
by limiting our response to intellectual comprehension
only, or by responding only if we hated the personality so
destroyed; but then the situation would not be comic, we
would not laugh if we only knew or hated. In order to
laugh we must accept the destruction of personality. Such
destructive effects may become acceptable, however,
through the artistry which produces a caricature or a parody; for if such artistry represents the human personality
as destroyed, it transforms the occasion of this destruction
into support of the formed-content of the art-work. The
personality destroyed is not reduced to its primitive elements, but to those elements as they can be presented in
the art-work. In the case of such a painting as Jack Levine's
Feast of Pure Reason for example, the greed, lust, and sensuality are depicted in such a way as to destroy the human
claims of the personalities represented, but they are still
the greed, lust, and sensuality presented in line and color,
in plane and paint, and not those of an alien nature itself.
In consequence they are acceptable.

The significance of this artistic presentation of the primitive in man in the terms of the art-work, is to be found in
the revelation of the limits of the personality which the
art-work sets in relief or shatters. The primitive elements
which, in caricature and parody, set in relief and shatter a
personality, bound it and reveal its limitations. The accept-
ability of these elements suggests that the personality
which is in fact bounded by them could be open to them;
that such primitive elements are alien aspects of the per-

sonality in which this self could participate, and in which the artist and appreciator do participate in the art-work. Yet the extent of this participation is restricted to those bestial, those primitive elements of human nature which are excluded from man's developed personality. A broader range of openness, of participation in the alien, is hardly attainable in caricature or parody. For this we must look to more complex examples of the comic; and, for purposes of illustration, let us choose the collective humor of the American Frontier. In this subject one can see, variously stated, the claim that the frontiersman, his nature set in relief and shattered by those alien circumstances constituting the frontier, can turn toward these and accept them, can participate in them.

Along the American Frontier, wherever it appeared and in whatever form it took, men found themselves committed to dealing with a strange and unexpected situation. When they moved out to the frontier, they may have envisaged their new life in terms of a projection of their aspirations and hopes. They probably did suppose that the life they were going to lead in the West was to be a life fulfilling their ambitions. The reality which confronted them in their log cabins, their sod huts, their adobe homes was so different, so alien as to appear unintelligible. It was an alien world, a new world in which they had come to live, and not a better extension of the old one. Perhaps the central function of frontier humor was to make this unbelievable fact explicit, and to suggest that this incredible world had something to offer man if he could come to accept it. This function was fulfilled with varying emphases. First, for example, there were advertisements for land in the

West, advertisements which were not quite serious—for while they appealed to prospective buyers in the terms of their old life and beliefs, they did so in such an exaggerated way as to suggest something more. Consider some quotations from an advertisement in *Bob Taylor's Magazine* in 1906, depicting the Nueces River Valley Paradise:

Where the flowers bloom ten months in the year;

Where something can be planted and harvested every month in the year;

Where the country is advancing and property values rapidly increasing;

Where there are no aristocrats and people do not have to work hard to have plenty and go in the best society;

Where the water is pure, soft and plentiful;

Where the laws protect both the investor and the settler;

Where the taxes are so low that the amount is never missed;

Where peace, plenty and good will prevail . . .

Where it is so healthy that people rarely die, except from accident . . .

Here the sweep of exaggeration is so full as to imply that the reality behind the rhetoric is different, and to imply that the prospective immigrant is interested in this even though he doesn't know it or explicitly admit it. The last reference to longevity was an old stand-by in frontier humor; it was often carried so far as to parody the hopes of the immigrants. For example,

But we have the healthiest climate in California. It is so healthy we had to shoot a man to start a graveyard.

In this the exaggeration is made unbelievable. Why? In order to refer more explicitly to the reality behind it, a strange and yet interesting reality. Other ways of making the same point are typical of the frontier, as the stories referring to the elephant.

> Among thousands of returning emigrants we passed one jovial party with a huge sketch of an elephant upon their wagon labeled: "What we saw at Pike's Peak."

By way of explanation of this often used symbol, E. B. Hathaway remarked,

> You hear the phrase used variously of these quitters that are heading back for Independence [Missouri] as: "They've seen too much of the Elephant," or "the Elephant's tracks got too close." In rare instances the continent is referred to as "the Elephant," and the continental divide ahead of us as the top of the Elephant's back.

But the reality of the American continent does not always remain hidden, for very often in American humor it is described as alien to man as well as unbelievable; yet the wryness, the humor which marks acceptance is always there.

> Of course it gets dry out there, they say, so dry sometimes that the cattle starve down and climb through the holes in the chicken wire, and hide among the chickens, and that's annoying.

> A drop of water hit a man, and they had to throw two buckets of dirt in his face to bring him to.

> This would be a fine country if we just had water . . . but then so would hell.

> In this country we climb for water and dig for wood.

In much of American humor, the incongruity of the old standards and ways of life with the new West was the base of reference; and the plea implicit in the humor is that the given alien character of the West has something to offer man. As Mark Twain said, "It seems a pity that the world should throw away so many good things just because they are unwholesome."

The point we have been exploring may be seen more clearly in the epitome of American Frontier humor, that of Mark Twain. At its best Mark Twain's art is not merely caricature or parody; he achieves mature comedy not by contrasting the genteel idealism of Eastern society and tradition with the reality of the frontier, but by placing man within the reality of the frontier, by revealing man as standing in this horizon and as accepting his place. Mark Twain's laughter is an affirmation of the shrewdness, the chicanery, the illusion and myopic vision, the partiality and diversity of the panorama of human effort as it was actually unfolding in the West Samuel Clemens knew so well. This laughter is graver than that of his fellow humorists: it is laughter at human expressions of value, at human ideals seen in the context of the Journey West, symbolized in one instance in the journey of Huck Finn down the Mississippi. Consider the laughter at the King in this story, who pretends to royalty on the American frontier, and who is the very symbol of that traditional human aspiration which the realities of the frontier make ludicrous and bring down to earth. Consider Mark Twain's admission of the democratic ground for these pretensions when the King says, "Hain't we got all the fools in town on our side? And ain't that a big enough majority in any town?" Yet in the end Mark Twain affirms human pretension and democratic confusion as essential to human life itself. It is Huck Finn, who says of the pitiful ending of royalty which he conscientiously brought about, ". . . I knowed it was the king and the duke, though they was all over tar and feathers and didn't look like nothing in the world that was human . . . and I was sorry for them poor pitiful rascals, it seemed like I couldn't ever feel any hardness against them . . . If I had a yaller dog that didn't know no more than a person's conscience does I would poison him. It takes up more room than all the rest of a person's insides and yet ain't no good, nohow."

The course of human life seen from the level of the current of the Mississippi is devious; from this perspective it is a congeries of human pretensions and illusions, vagaries, and distorted aspirations. That is, human life becomes a comedy when its setting in an alien nature is revealed. In Mark Twain's hands humor no longer marks merely the acceptance of the expression of the elemental in man as in caricature or parody; it is, rather, an affirmation of a participation which mirrors man's being not alone in the products of his efforts, in his immediate goods and values, but finds his being in the comedy of his partial, diverse, and conflicting enterprises. In Mark Twain's genius, humor is the human voice emerging in relation to an environment of a West it accepts, it is the human voice testifying that openness to the New World, an alien world, can be achieved in recognizing and laughing at the partiality and immediacy and distortion in human life. The laughter pealing through Mark Twain's art is a statement of man's openness; but a statement which finds this openness in man's membership

in the damned human race, so that Mark Twain could say
that when you achieve the ideal and enter heaven:

> Leave your dog outside. Heaven goes by favor. If it went by
> merit, you would stay out and the dog would go in.

For Samuel Clemens respect was gained for man not in
heaven but upon the dramatic journey of life, a journey in
which one could participate only by accepting the harsh
and alien realities of a frontier.

III. The Comedy of Appearance

A characteristic of early Chaplin comedies is the final scene
in which Charlie walks off down the road into the setting
sun. In some way Chaplin has gained our sympathy for
the character he portrays, and we respond positively, even
sentimentally, to this scene. But why is our response positive? Why should we accord to Charlie the right to walk
away from a situation which has rendered him powerless;
that is, the right to move with confidence out of a situation
in which he has acted with prototypical inadequacy in
trying to relate to the obstinate, non-human world around
him? This alien world reveals all of Charlie's acquired
traits and abilities to be impotent in dealing with it; yet it
leaves him curiously unbeaten. Curiously we say, for although he *is* beaten in every ordinary human way, he seems
to emerge from his lost battles as if he had won them in
some more fundamental sense. Evidently Chaplin wishes
to carry us to a new insight as he develops the successive
failures of Charlie in dealing with harsh circumstances
into the culminating movement down the road into the

setting sun. He develops this new insight partly through the sentimentality of the closing scene; yet we sense that this emotional response does not reflect the substance of the insight.

There is in Charlie's attitude toward each of his failures an odd openness, for since Charlie never learns from his experiences he is able to approach new circumstances with an ingenuous confidence which is difficult for *us*—who do learn from experience—to understand. Charlie is ever willing to respond to new situations as if he will be able to deal with them, acting out of the illusion of his competence with apparent conviction still once more. Of course it is clear to us that the only competence he really has is the competence of acting out this illusion. It is just this competence which is expressed in the integrity with which he wanders off, at the end, to face a never ending sequence of similar circumstances; for this act is an explicit admission on his part that any response he makes must always be, in this obvious sense, illusory. In a less obvious sense it is just the recognition of this illusion which affords him integrity. Charlie's specific failures would seem to have left him no integrity, yet he claims to have it. And he claims to have it, apparently, as a consequence of his willingness to proceed to live a life of illusion of which he is explicitly aware.

A man who is competent to judge his own illusions has achieved, at least, some openness. And Charlie goes beyond this basic achievement, for he suggests to us that he not only has some illusions, but that everything he does, all his responses, are illusions in some way. In achieving this he manages to claim, rightly, that he is open. His willingness to deal, without learning from the past, with each new circumstance suggests a fundamental openness to an alien world. The integrity he attains and expresses is the integrity of a man who realizes the importance of accepting even those circumstances which oppose him and controvert his own nature. The Charlie who walks off down the road is a man who intends to embrace the world in spite of what it has done and will do to him; a man who is open and supposes that he can remain open, a man who has achieved a radically new stage in the formation of his character. This is the substance of which his sentimentality is but an aspect.

In the early Chaplin comedies the alien world is presented in particular forms. Charlie tries after a tiring day to sleep in an in-a-door bed; or tries, on the point of starvation, to eat a boiled shoe. In these guises the alien appears as other than man, but it appears in a specific manifestation. In consequence, the illusory character of human response is related to these particular manifestations, and the expression of the possibility of overcoming illusion is limited by their particularity as well. That is, openness is attained in particular circumstances only. No doubt it is this restriction on openness which Chaplin wishes to transcend in the closing scene of his early comedies. There he wishes to suggest that the openness attained really is unrestricted and is a trait which can be maintained in any future circumstances. But this claim to transcendence to universal openness from particular instances is weak; hence the sentimentality of the scene. To express openness as a universal trait of man, it is necessary to present the alien world in the art-work in a general way, and not merely in a variety of its particular manifestations. To this end the alien character of the given, its otherness as such, must be formulated explicitly in the art-work. Because this formulation is not achieved in Chaplin's early comedies, the closing scene occasions our pathetic identification with Charlie and so a sentimental response rather than an acceptance of the other as such.

The problem of referring in a universal sense to what is other than man, and still present it as acceptable, has been solved in the forming techniques used in what might be called *comedies of appearance*. In these the very difficult problem of presenting the other in a general way is resolved by avoiding representing it at all. In these comedies universal otherness is symbolized as the indeterminate basis or ground for all pervasive human illusion. That is, all the perspectives of the protagonists are presented to provide a growing sense of the total unreality of the life the protagonists lead, so that in the end this life explodes in virtue of its compounded absurdity. The denouement is the suggestion of what makes this life unreal, the suggestion of the reality of that otherness against which life is revealed as illusion. This is suggested rather than detailed, implied rather than made explicit. Thus we come to see the protagonists as moving against the backdrop of an otherness which though neither understood nor formulated stands opposed to what is human, revealing man's perspectives as illusion; but which must be accepted because the only alternative would be to accept illusion. That is, man's openness is presented in a universal way because it is a turning away from general illusion to what is, without qualification, other than he is, the ground of this illusion.

In comedies of appearance laughter is incipient rather than overt, just as in them the other occurs as implicit rather than explicit. We laugh at particular given situations which—though revealing man as incompetent—we are able to accept. In comedies of appearance, when we turn to accept otherness in general in preference to illusion, our response is more complex than overt laughter. Our response is to become open, and becoming open is not so pointed as laughter; nor, probably, can it be characterized as any specific kind of response. When the veil of illusion explodes, finally, in a comedy of appearance, the protagonists respond by turning away from illusion toward, presumably, the other. Such an acceptance is forced upon them, and we as appreciators also come to accept from within our awareness of the horizon of their illusion. We would laugh, no doubt, if we could focus upon a specific point or situation; but our response is more universal. In fact, our acceptance is a recognition of our dignity as human beings; we accept because as men we have no alternative if we are to preserve our humanity; we accept out of the capacity of our humanity to be oriented toward the given and by accepting we make this capacity explicit. We cannot identify with our illusions, as we see; we must be open, and a comedy of appearance drives this home, making it possible for us to come to know what such openness is and means.

Eugene O'Neill's *Strange Interlude* is a comedy of appearance. Understood in these terms, the central line of development is the attempt of Nina to respond to the fact of her fiancé Gordon's death during the war, that is, to the fact that her human vision of happiness has been shattered. Throughout the play the modes of her response are presented as human efforts to deal with the shocking impact of Gordon's death. In her attempts to respond in human terms to the negative fact of the death—that is, to reconstitute her vision—she prostitutes herself, marries Sam, has a child by Darrell, raises this child, also named Gordon, as Sam's son, and finally marries Marsden. Each new response in this chain is elicited by a recurrence of the negative in the situation, a recurrence which requires a new response. Thus each response is a cry for human happiness. But while it is a *cry* evoked by the negative elements in experience, it is a cry which expresses the meaning and significance of the negative situation in human terms merely. Nina's responses gradually come to be understood as in contrast to the negative element which occasions them, and they thus gradually emerge as partial and illusory. From Nina's first attempts to find Gordon and her vision again in the torn bodies of soldiers in the hospital in which she is a nurse, we are aware of the irrelevance of her responses to the negative fact of Gordon's death. The strained and unreal character of this first response is developed in later responses as well. The involved relationship with Sam—and then with Darrell, in order to have a son Sam needs—is so complex as to be almost unbelievable. Similarly, the style of the play, with its expression of thought as well as conversation, its contrast of these "spoken" thoughts with ordinary conversation, and its psychoanalytic overtones, serves to elaborate the already great complexity of plot and to deepen the sense of unreality. Thus the play becomes more and more evidently a story of human responses revealed as illusions; and the denouement becomes an acceptance of that other which serves as the implicit standard of the judg-

ment of this illusion. At the end of the play Nina is able to
stand as open to that other which her all too human pursuit of happiness has driven her to disguise in more and
more elaborate illusions, illusions which are to be continued in the lives of her son and his wife, but which are ex-
punged in her life at this point near its end.

Nina calls, at the last, to her son Gordon, as he flies away
with his wife to continue the human response to the given,
to build illusion:

> NINA (*with tortured exultance*) : Fly up to heaven, Gordon!
> Fly with your love to heaven! Fly always! Never crash to
> earth like my old Gordon! Be happy, dear! You've got to be
> happy!

> DARRELL (*sardonically*) : I've heard that cry for happiness
> before, Nina! I remember hearing myself cry it—once—it
> must have been long ago! I'll get back to my cells—sensible
> unicellular life that floats in the sea and has never learned
> the cry for happiness! I'm going, Nina. (*As she remains ob-
> livious, staring after the plane—[he is] thinking fatalisti-
> cally*)

>> She doesn't hear, either . . .
>> (*He laughs up at the sky*)
>> Oh, God, so deaf and dumb and blind! . . . teach me
>>   to be resigned to be an atom!
> (*He walks off, right, and enters the house*).

Yet Darrell's sardonic comment is not really applicable, for
Nina, too, has projected her human preoccupation on her
son. She is now able to see the unreality of her struggles,
their incredible nature, and to turn to the occasion of them
without at once turning away from it and so be caught
again in the partiality and illusion of human fabrication:

NINA (*finally lowering her eyes—confusedly*): Gone. My eyes are growing dim. Where is Ned? Gone, too. and Sam is gone. They're all dead. Where are Father and Charlie? (*With a shiver of fear she hurries over and sits on the bench beside* [*Charlie*] *Marsden, huddling against him*) Gordon is dead, Father. I've just had a cable. What I mean is, he flew away to another life—my son, Gordon, Charlie. So we're alone again—just as we used to be.

. . . . .

NINA (*looking up at the sky—strangely*): My having a son was a failure wasn't it? He couldn't give me happiness. Sons are always their fathers.

. . . . .

MARSDEN (*paternally—in her father's tone*): You had best forget the whole affair of your association with the Gordons. After all, dear Nina, there was something unreal in all that has happened since you first met Gordon Shaw, something extravagant and fantastic, the sort of thing that isn't done, really, in our afternoons. So let's you and me forget the whole distressing episode, regard it as an interlude of trial and preparation, say, in which our souls have been scraped clean of impure flesh and made worthy to bleach in peace.

NINA (*with a strange smile*): Strange interlude! Yes, our lives are merely strange dark interludes in the electrical display of God the Father! (*Resting her head on his shoulder*) You're so restful, Charlie. . . . It will be a comfort to get home—to be old and to be home again at last— . . . to die in peace! I'm so contentedly weary with life!

In these last speeches Nina is able to turn away from the merely human cry for happiness just because her cry turns into a cry for lost happiness. Yet her awareness of the loss is grounded in her sense of the illusions into which the pursuit of happiness has led her, so that she turns from this pursuit willingly. Toward what? Toward something which, however ambiguously stated as Gordon's death, as "unicellular life," as "atoms," as an "electrical display," is other than the human desire for happiness or any human desire. Nina turns toward this willingly, now open to it, realizing that it has something to offer her, something which may be adumbrated, if also falsified, in such human terms as rest and contentment.

In a comedy of appearance, the central pivot is the turning of the chief protagonists from illusion, explicitly recognized, to what is other than man. What is other than man, usually presented as negative elements in an art-work, emerges in such comedy first as the illusory quality of appearance, and then as that which is an alternative to illusion. We become aware of the motives, the beliefs, the activities of the protagonists as illusions because the artist enables us to see through them and around them. We do not see the other as such; but we do become aware of it as in opposition to the points of view and responses the protagonists develop. Any form of comedy recognizes the need to take account of the other, of what is not human, in such a way as to relate man to it, and so to reveal its contribution to the art-work. The greater merit of a comedy of appearance is that when the artist unrolls and makes explicit the panorama of human illusion, he makes it laughable and allows us to accept it as illusory by suggesting that openness to what is other than man reveals that an aesthetic occasion has the other as well as man as a source.

The achievement of such openness of character in ordinary life is difficult and often impossible, for in life openness often seems to require the acceptance of literally unacceptable circumstances. In art the givenness of the medium is sensed already as according to the art-work a contribution necessary for its development. The function of the forming in any comedy, but especially in a comedy of appearance, is to formulate this giving on the part of the given in such a way as to make it clear that the possibility of disclosing content depends upon it. This generality may be achieved, as we have seen, by depicting the protagonists in a comedy as open to what is alien; that is, as participating in a process to which the other makes a contribution. Since this depiction is developed in the terms of a medium which accords a contribution to the art-work, the openness depicted has this support, and in consequence it can carry the artist (and the appreciator) into an aesthetic occasion as participators in a process in which the other, transmuted, also participates. Thus through the artist and the appreciator art is revealed as incorporating what is not man.

CHAPTER 5

TRANSCENDENTAL FORM: TRAGEDY

I. *Intuition of the Hero*

In a comedy or comic situation man as a protagonist or as an appreciator accepts capricious events, he goes along with them come what may. We recall of a comedy a sense of the participation of the protagonists in the flow of events, that they were carried along in the rush; and, in consequence, we recall our own appreciative identification with the turns of the wheel of fortune. In comedy we are caught up by the other and we accept it; our awareness is not brought to focus upon the individuality of the protagonists or ourselves. In the tragic sense of life, or in a tragedy, by contrast, it is man who holds our attention as he brings himself to stand before the other. So much so, indeed, that we recall tragic art by the name of the hero who becomes the symbol for it. It is as if the fool, the simpleton, of a comedy were irradiated and transfigured so as to take the center of the tragic stage. It is as if man, having identified himself with the rush of circumstance, and having been engulfed by it, had emerged from this baptism in the alien with a new and more significant character. We sense in tragedy the emergence of the hero, and, indeed, this emergence has been portrayed often as a kind of epiphany. In consequence, we commonly think of the tragic hero as a person of great stature, as one whose character develops sharply and violently. The understanding of man's character as heroic in this sense can lead to the heart of tragedy; but, as we shall see, the tragic hero may be presented in terms of almost pure misery and suffering, as he often is in modern works. Still, whatever he is, it is the hero who defines tragedy.

Let us begin our consideration of tragedy with some simple situations which are called tragic. Through an examination of these we may hope to fix an intuition of the tragic, to elicit some essential elements which may serve as a base line for a survey of more complex and more profound structures within tragedy.

If we hear about a man diving into a raging torrent to try to rescue a drowning child and dying in the attempt, we commonly call the situation tragic. We say this in part, no doubt, because we see the terrible forces of nature conquering man. But we say it not only on this account, but also because the man in this situation has acted in such a way as to defy these forces. We see man as agent certain to be engulfed by insuperable natural odds, but plunging into them none the less. Thus we envision the agent as a hero who stands forth in the midst of a terrifying and hopeless situation.

In some situations, mildly tragic, the protagonist himself develops in such a way as to stand forth, so that we see the situation as tragic through his eyes. This may happen, for example, when an old man, nearing the end of his life, looks back upon its course and reviews its turmoil and conflict, the hates and passions which filled it, its successes and failures. Of course this review may plunge him back into a kind of vicarious reliving of his life, but it need not. At this time his will is quiet, he has little to live for, and in a sense his life is over. This may help him to see himself as having lived the terror of a human history, to see himself as having been caught up in the course of the world. He may sum up his life, may manage to take an impartial and comprehensive view of the past, and emerges in consequence as a heroic figure.

In negative circumstances, in circumstances which entail his destruction, the agent in a tragic situation stands forth, refusing to be conquered. He responds to negative circumstances by opposing them in a special way. His response is quite different from that suggested by Whitman when he says:

> I make the poem of evil also—I commemorate that part also
> I am myself as much evil as good, and my nation is—
> And I say there is in fact no evil.

The ego in this poem is presented as identifying with the negative, is presented as participating in the whole which includes it. This ego is no tragic hero; for such a hero responds in a way suggested by Hermann Melville, when he says in *Moby Dick*:

> Delight is to him . . . a far, far upward and inward delight
> —who against the proud gods and commodores of this earth,
> ever stands forth, his own inexorable self.

Evidently part of what we commonly mean when we speak of a tragic situation includes a hero who faces the hopelessness and terror of the circumstances in which he finds himself. Indeed, our sense of the stature of the hero is so deep that we may make too much of it and take his greatness as the key to tragedy. We may be led to conceive of the hero as transcending the circumstances which destroy him. This is hardly his significance.

To understand the significance of the hero in tragedy we must note that his emergence takes place within the con-

text of artistic activity. It is our artistic, selective response
to the circumstance of a man's death in the effort to save a
drowning child which develops the tragic. The situation becomes a tragic one as we interpret it to include negative
elements, and as our comprehension of the agent's character develops so that we see him standing forth. Not all old
men, indeed only a few of them, come at the end of their
lives to stand in a tragic situation. For to achieve this, they
must come to see the course of their lives as taking place in
the matrix of negative circumstances, as leading to inevitable death; and they must come to see themselves as emerging in this context as confronting life rather than as
participating in it. Their life achieves the dignity of tragedy, that is, in and through their interpretive responses to
its literal events and circumstances. It is a kind of artistic
response to circumstances by a participant (or on the part
of an observer) which develops or selects the patterns of a
context having a tragic structure, and it is a mistake to suppose that any element in this structure, for example the
hero, can be understood apart from it. When we come to
view a courageous man's attempt at rescue as the act of a
hero, we also come to see those circumstances which destroy him as contributing to the development of the artistic
patterns of tragedy. Similarly, the old man who sums up his
life in a certain way enters, as he does so, a developing artistic context in which those circumstances which will destroy him are seen as contributing to this structure.

What is meant here may be seen more clearly, perhaps,
where there is art present in an explicit sense. Let us consider the autobiography of Henry Adams, a *book* which we

read and to which we respond. Henry Adams tells us he began his adult life with faith in human nature and faith in
science. He believed that power could be harnessed for the
benefit of man. As his life developed he found his illusions
slipping away, his hopes for a political career and accomplishment disappearing, his aspirations to achieve the social
expression of human value frustrated. He says that he
found the human mind stripped naked, vibrating in a void
of shapeless energies and wasted and destroyed by them.
He came to feel, he says, that in the nineteenth century
there was nothing real but the expression of power without
an aim. In a word, he came to view modern culture as opposing man, as the embodiment of forces and powers which
contributed nothing to man and would end by destroying
him. In the face of what he regarded as the inevitable doom
for mankind Adams raises his voice in the depiction of the
situation as he sees it. He states and dwells upon this situation in an expression of despair; but it is an expression in
which Adams emerges as the voice of this despair; it is an
expression by the human voice echoing against blind power
and chaos, brought to being in response to them.

The human voice Adams raises is the voice of the artist,
and the art-work which his autobiography makes available
to us comes to be out of this echo reflected from blind
power and chaos. It is an art-work, that is, which Adams'
tragic despair serves to reveal as developing from its source
in what is alien and opposed to man. There is a different
disclosure of content because Adams depicts shapeless
powers wasting man, and because the voice he raises in the
face of them is the voice of an artist; for in this way Adams

opens the path into an aesthetic occasion which clearly has its roots in the alien, which clearly develops in relation to this.

The point just made concerning the place of the art-work is exemplified in a much different way in the Chinese poet Po Chü-i's "Last Poem." The translation by Arthur Waley reads:

They have put my bed beside the unpainted screen;
They have shifted my stove in front of the blue curtain.
I listen to my grandchildren reading me a book;
I watch the servants heating up my soup.
With rapid pencil I answer the poems of friends,
I feel in my pockets and pull out medicine-money.
When this superintendence of trifling affairs is done,
I lie back on my pillows and sleep with my face to the South.

The circumstances which oppose man are introduced very obliquely and very indirectly into the poem. They are hinted at, suggested, by the activities and circumstances of an old man. But we hardly become aware of the significance of these activities and this situation until the last line of the poem tells us that Po Chü-i faces death. Then the fact that a man has been brought to the end of his life and that this end is unavoidable is presented to us. And this fact confronts Po Chü-i as well. It is to this fact that Po Chü-i, as a figure in the poem, responds with human dignity; he composes himself, and awaits his fate. But this is not quite all, for we know that he responded to the circumstances confronting him in another way as well: he wrote his "Last Poem," as he calls it. The poem itself reflects the same sense of human dignity in the face of death as do the acts the poet depicts within the poem. The poem itself portrays the fact of human mortality with restraint, and it affords a mode of response to this fact which states man's dignity in the face of it. The poem, however, is a mode of response which has its source in those facts which condemn man; and it is a mode of response which incorporates them, which discloses through them a content in which man, too, participates.

In Adams' autobiography and in Po Chü-i's final poem, the fact that the artist is depicting himself introduces an ambiguity which aids in developing the structure of the art-work as tragic. The hero of the poem is depicted as confronting those unavoidable circumstances which will destroy him, and he takes his stand before them. At this level there is no resolution. But the hero is also the poet, and the poem develops in response to those circumstances which destroy the poet. He and we enter a different art-work, this poem, because Po Chü-i raises his voice in the face of circumstances, and his voice is the voice of an artist. The poet opens a path into an aesthetic occasion which has a source in what is alien to man, what is other than man; an aesthetic occasion which is sustained in the terms of this alien source.

Before developing the analysis of the tragic, let us recapitulate. In the first place, in a tragedy negative elements are presented directly and with emphasis. They are depicted as powerful enough to engulf and destroy the protagonist. In the second place, there is a hero, that is, a man who develops in such a way as to stand forth confronting the negative circumstances, but whose development none the less reflects the sustaining contribution of these circumstances to the art-work. In the third place, the hero moves as a figure in an art-work in which the negative circumstances support and sustain the disclosure of content.

II. Man's Fate

Evidently, the protagonists in a tragedy find themselves caught up in the coursing of events which destroy them. But if this is an essential part of a tragedy, it is so because of a complex pattern which gives to the destruction its peculiarly tragic meaning. As evidently as the negative circumstances in a tragedy destroy the hero, there is art in which the destruction of the protagonists takes place without raising the action to the level of tragedy. Flaubert's *Madame Bovary* is a pivotal work in respect to this point. In this novel Madame Bovary's circumstances and her character produce her downfall. Indeed, with her character and under the circumstances in which she finds herself, the end is inevitable. The circumstances are those of a mean provincial society; her character is no worse than that of many middle class people in that society; yet because of both she becomes a victim of circumstances, for she can neither escape them nor change her own nature. The novel is impressive, but is it a tragedy? Does the account of Madame Bovary's destruction have the complex pattern which is found in tragedy? No doubt she is destroyed because of what she is, but can we say that what she is is different from the events which destroy her? Is her destruction an inevitable accident, a mere consequence of the character which she happens (accidentally) to have? In a word, is Madame Bovary the heroine of a tragedy?

138

Madame Bovary is an instance of a trend in the style of modern and contemporary tragedies—if they are to be called that. It seems possible to call Madame Bovary miserable and to recapitulate the pattern of her life by calling it pathetic. This is possible in Hemingway's *A Farewell to Arms* also, where the chief protagonist announces the intent of his story at the beginning of his account of the retreat from Caporetto:

> I was always embarrassed by the words sacred, glorious, and sacrifice and the expression in vain. . ,. . We had heard them, . . . and had read them . . . now for a long time, and I had seen nothing sacred, and the things that were glorious had no glory and the sacrifices were like the stockyards at Chicago if nothing was done with the meat except to bury it.

Catherine's description of her own imminent death expresses the same tone:

> "I'm going to die," she said; then waited and said, "I hate it" . . . Then a little later, "I'm not afraid. I just hate it" . . . "Don't worry, darling, . . . I'm not a bit afraid. It's just a dirty trick."

Painful and pitiful death, certainly. An account of misery and death, of course. But could this be an instance of the death of a tragic hero? And could the intent of the book be consistent with tragedy?

Madame Bovary, A Farewell To Arms, Ibsen's *Ghosts* are examples of modern and contemporary art which is often termed tragic art; but they seem to differ in structure from earlier tragedies. The evident difference between this art and earlier tragedies like *Oedipus the King* or *Hamlet* lies in the contrast between the character of the heroes.

There is some justice in observing that earlier tragedies depict their heroes as having great souls, as splendid, as standing out amid the forces that destroy them and transcending these forces. By contrast modern works are accounts of despair, of misery, even of human distress; accounts, moreover, which are not alleviated by the nobility of their heroes. Modern critics have noted that ancient tragedy deals almost exclusively with kings and courts, and they often recall that Aristotle said, "Tragedy is an imitation of persons who are above the common level . . ." And they are led to conclude that only such works are tragedies; whereas modern works, although similar in structure, fail to be tragedies just because they fail to ennoble, fail to accord to their heroes that stature which somehow places them beyond the reach of those circumstances which destroy them.

Yet if one quotes Aristotle one must add to his comments about the character of the protagonists his statement that character is subsidiary in tragedy. He says, "without action there cannot be a tragedy; there may be without character." And one should recall that the definition of tragedy which he gives does not refer to character: "Tragedy, then, is an imitation of an action that is serious, complete and of a certain magnitude . . . Tragedy is an imitation, not of men, but of an action and of life . . ." Evidently, Aristotle found the core of tragedy elsewhere than in the grandeur of human character. And, indeed, while it is true that the nobility of many classical heroes has something to tell us about tragedy, it is also true that the misery and the pitiful deaths of ordinary men in modern works does not, of itself, prevent them from *acting* in a tragedy nor from being the hero of it.

The heroes of modern tragedies may serve as the occasion for reconsidering the nature of tragedy and the place of the hero in tragedy. Those modern heroes whose fate is syphilis, as Oswald Alving in *Ghosts* or the hero of Thomas Mann's *Dr. Faustus;* those modern heroes whose misery overcomes them so that they die without grandeur, or whose death is symbolic, a death of the soul and a kind of extermination of hope; these heroes may serve to reveal something of the structure of tragedy which we might otherwise miss or under-emphasize. Very likely, the insight of the creators of modern tragedy is just this; they see the need of a different hero, because by emphasizing misery and suffering they may focus our attention upon a significance of tragedy which might otherwise be lost to us through the attraction for us of those splendid figures who are the heroes of older tragedies. But that to which they would recall us is to be found in the older tragedies as well. The essential movement of a tragedy is not the development of the character of a man so that we exult and glory in the greatness of his soul even at the moment of death. We may feel passionate admiration for the hero of a tragedy, of course; but although this may enhance the art, it is not peculiar to tragedy. The essence of a tragic hero is to be found in the depiction of those activities through which man comes, as essentially human, to confront what is alien to him, and through which he is brought under the necessity of accepting the contribution of the other in the face of his human demands, though it destroy him.

A part of the significance of this distinction may be seen in the ways in which the artist introduces negative elements into the pattern of the art-work. First, he does this as forci-

bly as he can. He never attenuates the horror and terror of
the circumstances he depicts in their effects on man. Sophocles in *Oedipus the King* dwells upon paricide and incest,
the two horrors which engulf his hero. In *Hamlet* Shakespeare depicts the impact upon a son of the fact that the
murderer of his father is married to his mother. In O'Neill's
Desire Under the Elms the desire of the son for his father's
wife is consummated and leads to the wife's murder of
their child. One result of such compounding of horror is
to force us to consider such acts as monstrous, to force us
to comprehend them as having been brought about by
forces outside man. Certainly the evils resulting from lust,
or greed, or other vices may be grasped as humanly moti-
vated; but there are actions which can have no such motivation, which if they occur can be accounted for only in
the terms of man's domination by uncharted currents and
unknown levels of existence. The man who commits incest, the woman who murders her children are beside themselves; they act from sources which do not fall within the
horizons of humanity. Through the horror of such acts we
come to see that such people must be torn and twisted by
external currents, that they must be moved by what to
them is as alien and overpowering as their acts seem to us.
By the depiction of what is morally inconceivable, the artist presents his protagonists as having been wrenched out
of their human context and nature and buffeted by an alien
sea in which everything human floats precariously.

Emphasis in a tragedy upon the most terrible moral
transgressions aids the artist in setting the protagonists in
the context of what lies beyond man. But this emphasis
also serves to bring to explicit awareness what is peculiarly

human; it focuses attention upon what man is. A tragedy written in the terms of incest, or of paricide, or of the murder of children reflects not only the fact that man fails to maintain his standards; it reflects, too, the fact that as a moral agent man has no recourse but to hold to these standards. These humanly impossible transgressions are just those terrible distortions into which man's action falls because he will not yield, he can not forego the standards which define his humanity. We see in the distortion of such actions the very edge of humanity; and because we see the edge, we see the internal structure of man's nature all the more clearly. We see, that is, man's nature as demands made upon the alien circumstances which he confronts.

In this sense, the movement of the hero in a tragedy is a movement to the limits which define humanity itself. And this bounding of his nature has the significance of a flaw or defect. In Goethe's portrayal of Faust, Faust comes to be defined in the terms of man's desire for knowledge; his nature develops to become that of man. Faust becomes a symbol expressing the unavoidable human demand that the world fall within finite human comprehension. In the desire of Faust for knowledge we see him as man, the lines defining human nature drawn; and through this lens we see, as well, beyond him to what opposes and destroys him.

What was Othello's defect? He tells us himself:

> Speak of me as I am; nothing extenuate,
> Nor set down ought in malice; then must you speak
> Of one that loved, not wisely, but too well;

Yet is it a defect to love? Certainly not when viewed from within the human horizon, for it is man's nature to focus upon the particular, and to become passionately attached to it. But loving person or place or idea too well is to push to the bounds of human eros, to reveal this as it is, as limited; and so as set within what is alien to it and opposes it. Loving too well does not, however, deny that love characterizes man.

In Sophocles' *Oedipus the King* it is Creon who tells Oedipus, as all is lost:

Crave not mastery in all, For the mastery that raised thee was thy bane and wrought thy fall.

Mastery of this or that, of course; but to desire mastery of all is to commit the sin of pride. Yet without mastery what is man? The limning of man's nature as a mastering develops from particular occurrences in Oedipus' history which are referred to in the action of the play. Thus we come to know that before Oedipus' birth an oracle foretold that he would kill his father and marry his mother. When Oedipus is born his father, the king Laius, acts to forestall the predicted event; he has the child's legs bound and orders him to be exposed. Acting within the limits of human competence, what else could he do? Yet Oedipus escapes this death. And Oedipus himself, when he later learns that he is to kill his father and marry his mother, leaves his foster parents in order to avoid this fate. The play, at this level, is a history of human action, competent and effective action, such as that through which Oedipus eventually becomes king of Thebes and solves the riddle of the Sphinx. He becomes, that is, just that paradigm of human competence, who, seeking to deal with the plague threatening his city, is capable of finding the man who is responsible for it.

As Oedipus rises to the task of discovering the man responsible for the plague (that is, himself) he begins to loom as larger than a particular individual engaged upon specific tasks. He emerges as an archetype of *human* action; he discovers not only himself, but man.

We come to see the king as a person whose movements are not accidental, but autonomous and necessary. His motivation to mastery emerges as the very nature of man; *and* as a movement which cannot be set aside or altered. Oedipus himself suggests the justifiable character of this movement when he compares himself with Apollo, the god of light. It is Oedipus who tells Tiresias when the seer refers to his crimes:

> Offspring of endless Night, thou hast no power
> O'er me or any man who sees the sun.

In this relation to Apollo Oedipus claims for his nature a legitimacy which cannot be denied. As the outlines of his nature become clear in Oedipus' actions, the limits of human competence are revealed in its results, paricide and incest. As Oedipus moves to the very limits of his nature he is engulfed by the impossible darkness which surrounds it. But at this moment, as he drives the pins of his wife-mother's brooches through his eyeballs, he reaffirms his nature, man's nature, as it condemns him to the darkness engulfing it.

Sophocles presents Oedipus as a man of light, as exacting clarity, as a demander of explicitness. He presents him, that is, not as an ordinary personality but as an archetype. He presents him as required by the legitimacy of his demand to develop to his limits as a man and so to stand open to the alien circumstances which underlie him. In this encounter with what is to be found beyond the horizon of his awareness he falls into the distorting power of the inscrutable forces of the Titans, for he extends his actions beyond recognizable form. And having come to this encounter, he affirms the development which led him to this bound, this death. The moment of tragedy is the moment when Oedipus—having moved beyond his ordinary personality to stand as a legitimate demander of light—confronts the impossible darkness he would penetrate, and affirms both his need and his right to stand there. Strictly speaking, the hero of a tragedy is this pattern of action; whatever else he may be is an elaboration upon this movement.

Shakespeare's *Hamlet,* too, is the story of an individual who is placed in circumstances which force him to realize to the fullest what his nature is—and to find it lacking. The situation which forces Hamlet to begin to limn his own nature is, of course, the revelation (by the ghost) of the fact that the murderer of Hamlet's father is now married to Hamlet's mother. In such a circumstance Hamlet is presented with an incredible situation, one which, if he ever comes to believe it, can be described only by saying that the course of life has been wrenched from its normal channel. Yet this circumstance requires a response, as Hamlet recognizes in saying:

> The time is out of joint: O cursed spite,
> That ever I was born to set it right!

In his first attempts at a response he tries to deal with the cataclysm as if it were a normal event in ordinary life. He seeks to deal with it in terms of his acquired personality, the terms which have accrued to him through his education and the building of his character. In consequence, he cannot believe it; he seeks to find out if it is true. He thinks about it, exercises his ingenuity to find out more about it, strives to come to some conclusion about it. Evidencing great ingenuity, he stages the play within the play; but even after this has established the truth that Claudius did kill his father, Hamlet still cannot act in terms appropriate to this fact. At the crucial moment calling for violence, he says:

> Now might I do it pat, now he is praying;
> And now I'll do't: and so he goes to heaven:
>
> .   .   .   .
>
> A villain kills my father; and for that,
> I, his sole son, do this same villain send
> To heaven.

Here the required violence is stopped by thought and Hamlet does nothing, can do nothing at the level of action required. Thus we are brought gradually to see that no matter how Hamlet exercises the ordinary resources of his personality so that he may respond to the extraordinary deflection of history which has occurred, his response will not be adequate. The forces which have set the time out of joint, which have wrenched history from its course, cannot be set right through any development of the ordinary responses of which Hamlet is capable.

Yet if Hamlet is unable to deal with the situation which confronts him, neither can Claudius any longer deal with Hamlet. Claudius' attempts to do so culminate in the banishment of Hamlet to England. Claudius intends to have him killed there. But Hamlet miraculously escapes death and returns. At this point Hamlet is not to be overcome by the ordinary powers of other individuals. If he has not transcended the bounds of his own personality and so come to act in a truly extraordinary way he has at least defined these bounds, come to be aware of his limits, to be able to stand upon these limits, and to some extent to see beyond them. Through this he has made himself safe from the plotting of Claudius, preserving himself for his fate.

What is revealed in this definition of Hamlet's bounds is something which is not merely accidental, not merely contingent; but which is humanity itself. As Hamlet plumbs the depths of his personality, pushes towards its boundaries and defines its limits, he limns not his acquired personality, but the nature of man; a transcendental nature which stands beyond the reach of Claudius or of any of the accidents of an ordinary human life. Thus if Hamlet is still powerless before the horrors which confront him, *this* limitation, *this* flaw, is not to be understood as an inability to cope with ordinary circumstance; this flaw must be understood as a characteristic of man and, as such, a fundamental inability to deal with the primordial forces which wrench history from its course and control his destiny.

Returning from England Hamlet comes upon an open grave. We know it to be Ophelia's, but he does not. He is forced, thus, to meditate upon death; and because of his ignorance, he meditates upon death in general, as a human fate, rather than upon this particular death and its specific circumstances. He sees in the open grave the destruction of

148

Caesar and of all men. At this moment, having moved already to the very edge of his nature, Hamlet begins to see beyond this limit, begins a different kind of encounter with the alien, which up to now he has tried to deal with only in *his* terms. Learning that this is Ophelia's grave he is pulled into it. He thus reenacts an age-old myth that man is led to cross the threshold into the extraordinary realm by means of love; and he emerges from the grave as having done this, as a different being, for he says:

> . . . This is I, Hamlet the Dane.
> . . . have I in me something dangerous,
> which let thy wisdom fear, Hold off thy hand.

Hamlet has buried in the grave of Ophelia his ordinary personality, and emerges, he feels, as an agent whose acts flow from his participation in the ground of history. As such an agent he acts with confidence, acts as if the terror and horror with which he must deal could be set right.

For a moment we seem to see Hamlet as a new and kinglike figure—in the words of Horatio:

> Why, what a king is this!

Yet he is no such king. Indeed, as we are told, a kinglike Hamlet never appears on the level of the action of the story at all. It is Fortinbras who observes of the dead Hamlet:

> Let four captains bear Hamlet, like a soldier, to the stage; for he was likely, had he been put on, to have proved most royally . . .

The Hamlet who wrenched history back upon its course did not come to exist as a kinglike man; that is, he acted

149

only through the forces which had set the time out of joint in the first place.

Hamlet died willingly, for—pursuing the hope that he could find within his personality the means for dealing with the terrible situation confronting him—he was led to break this personality in the course of this impossible, self-appointed task. His death, in this sense, is the death of his personality, a sacrifice of this in order to participate in those forces which could transmute his acts into the violent and alien movements required by the circumstances which confronted him. Hamlet's death is also the death of man, as such, for in his efforts to extend the bounds of his nature, he reveals what man is and so inscribes him. He sets man's limits, and so shows both what man's nature is and that man's nature needs to stand in relation to what is alien to man and will destroy him. In this sense Hamlet's death is that of a hero, for it points to the possibility of man's participation in that in which the alien also participates. What might happen in this participation the hero does not know; but that something will happen he does know. And he knows that he must open himself to, must put himself at the disposal of the forces which could bring this to be—even though if he does this, he will die for it. The long struggle of his development as a hero brings Hamlet to stand as a man, destined to set right the movement of those forces which have wrenched history from its course, in acts which require his acceptance of the alien ground of history, in acts which move toward the sacrifice of his human nature to demonstrate the continuous support, by what is alien to man, of what is ultimate.

III. The Heroic Movement

The hero is an essential part of a tragedy, yet who is he? How are we to conceive of that Oedipus who willingly moved into exile, of that Hamlet who might have taken the stage? To put the question in this way is to make it difficult, if not impossible, to answer; for this question assumes that the hero has come into being as a great soul, as a personality of noble stature. And, of course, the artist may have suggested this.

The artist may present the hero as standing at the point which connects the realm of human history and a realm beyond this, the point which connects time and the timeless. Many tragedies contain somewhat obscure references to a transcendent realm which the hero seems to represent and in which the hero may seem to take a place upon his death. In Sophocles' *Oedipus at Colonnus* we find the hero living in the wood of the Furies and refusing to depart from his rest in this sacred land. When he moves, in this drama, toward his death, he seems to die transfigured. And in Milton's *Samson Agonistes* there is a suggestion that Samson is the representative of God among His enemies. T. S. Eliot in *Murder in the Cathedral* permits Becket to say at the end of Part I:

> I know
> What yet remains to show you of my history
> Will seem to most of you at best futility,
> Senseless self-slaughter of a lunatic,
> Arrogant passion of a fanatic.

Yet the play is affirmative, and the implication of the chorus is that Becket is a saint.

In tragedies such as these there is the suggestion that the futility, the misery and suffering, the destruction of the hero come about because he represents an oracle or some transcendent order whose patterns are beyond ordinary understanding. That is, a hero who acts in terms of such an order must be destroyed by the patterns of the ordinary world. But even in such affirmative tragedies, the suggestion of the relation of the hero to a transcendent order is not unambiguous. If the suggestion of the chorus in *Murder in the Cathedral* is that Becket is a saint, this will not be found in any single comment, but only in the cumulative impact of the whole of its comments. This point is well put by Stephen Dedalus' dictum on tragedy in James Joyce's *Portrait of the Artist as a Young Man*:

> Aristotle has not defined pity and terror. I have. Pity is the feeling which arrests the mind in the presence of whatsoever is grave and constant in human sufferings and unites it with the human sufferer. Terror is the feeling which arrests the mind in the presence of whatsoever is grave and constant in human sufferings and unites it with the secret cause.

If, in a tragedy, there is an implication that the hero represents an ultimate order, this order remains inscrutable; it is not really comprehended. Joyce's observation that the cause of tragedy is secret is of the essence; for if the drama were to be given a setting in the transcendent order, if the hero were to be a figure moving clearly at that level, there could be no tragedy. Yet if this setting is unclear, the nobility and stature of the hero remain unclear as well.

The suggestion that the hero is a representative of a

higher order evidently emphasizes the significance of the hero; but since it is and must be a veiled suggestion one must accept such an account as elliptical. The artist may use another device for enhancing our sense of the significance of the hero. Thus he may depict the hero as coming to recognize the fate he approaches. The hero may be shown as developing through his own efforts and powers to this final awareness. When this development culminates, the consciousness of his fate seems to comprise a unity which defines and ennobles the hero. The paradigm of such a figure is Oedipus. Certainly in his case we see how a series of acts directed toward the discovery of the source of the plague comes to be bathed with the significance and horror of his discovery that *he* is this source. We do see this awareness as a culmination, and we regard Oedipus' achievement as a sign of his great stature.

The unity of the self-knowledge Oedipus achieves ennobles him. Yet a similar moment of awareness cannot be found in most tragedies. Even though Hamlet announces a new identity when he emerges from Ophelia's grave as a hero, this identity is not that attained through self-knowledge—for Hamlet is aware of his predicament almost from the first moments of the play. And Racine's heroine, Phèdre, develops no sense of her position; she is well aware of it as the play opens. Ahab in *Moby Dick* seems to go down quite blindly. Evidently, the moment of recognition can serve to emphasize the significance of the hero; but it does not define the hero.

Yet if neither the nobility of an individual having a place in a transcendent order nor the consciousness of fate is the determining property of a hero, how is he to be recognized? How can we as appreciators know the hero, or the artist as creator outline the hero? Underlying any suggestions of the hero's noble character, and present even where these do not occur, is a complex movement which carries the chief protagonist willingly (perhaps with growing awareness) to the limits of his distinctively human nature, a movement which leaves him at this limit at the mercy of the alien circumstances which surround him. We may say that the hero of a tragedy is just *this* movement, that by the hero we mean this kind of action. That is, the hero becomes a symbol for these actions, and we see that to grasp the nature of the heroic we must examine the way the artist portrays such action.

It is characteristic of heroic action that it leads to destruction and that this is to be the fate of the hero. The movement of the hero toward his fate is not presented as an act of his will. On the contrary, it is portrayed as a course of events affording no choice; the hero is depicted as acting from grounds of his nature which are so fundamental as to be beyond changing. Oedipus' drive toward mastery or Phèdre's consuming passion cannot admit of change; these must develop and so seal their fates. But there is also a quality of affirmation in heroic action, something the artist suggests and reinforces by veiled reference to the hero's nobility or to his great stature.

In tragedy this suggestion is veiled and does not permit a resolution of the paradox of affirming an action which leads to destruction. At least no resolution seems possible at the level of the hero's action and in terms of that context in which he acts. The paradox may be resolved, however, if the heroic movement is understood as a form of the tragic drama, rather than as characterizing an individual. Thus, from the point of view of the artist who develops the art-work there is no paradox in the fact that *he* depicts the hero as moving along a course leading to destruction, and that in developing this form, in writing the tragedy, this action is affirmed. Histrionically, within the tragedy, the action of the hero leads inevitably to destruction; but the delineation of the heroic movement by the artist constitutes an affirmation of this movement, as such. And through it there is an affirmation by any appreciator of the drama as well.

When the artist attributes nobility to the hero, when he implies that the hero might be a representative of a transcendent realm, he reflects within the symbolism of the story the significance of his telling it. Such devices as this may lead to confusion; but they need not, if they retain sufficient ambiguity of reference so that they cannot be taken literally. If this ambiguity is present, the quality of affirmation conveyed cannot be located *within* the drama, but adheres to the drama as a developing art-work. When these devices are used in this way, they convey the same significance as does the incorporation of historical materials into a tragedy. Many tragedies have a history; that is, they retell an old story, or repeat a myth, or constitute an artistic interpretation of events which have occurred in the past. The many versions of Faust's story are an evident instance of this; Shakespeare's *Julius Caesar* is another. But there are also a variety of tragic dramas where different characters, locales, and historical periods obscure common heroic movements: apparently different tragedies may have in common a theme of consuming passion, or a desire for mastery, or a symbolic human weakness. In such cases, the repetition of a theme, whether this repetition is explicit or not, becomes significant in the art-work. Such repetition underlines the fact that the heroic action presented is being affirmed in the art-work, since the artist, certainly, and the appreciator, most likely, are aware that an ancient theme has been selected for restatement. This kind of repetition is unambiguous, for it locates the affirmation of the destruction of the hero in the artistic enterprise. It makes clear the fact that the heroic movement is a part of the forming movement of the art-work, that dynamic realm in which the artist (and appreciator) may come to live and move and have his aesthetic being.

If this distinction resolves the paradox, it still leaves open the further question as to the function of the heroic movement as a forming movement leading to disclosure of content in the art-work.

Although the heroic movement is a relatively abstract form, we may come to see its function by recalling the function of much simpler and more specific forms in art. Underlying this complex pattern of a tragedy are the intrinsic rhythm and stress patterns of the prose or poetry which martial the words for our review, so that they appear with an uncommon aura and intensity which they could never have without these. The use of rhyme, rhythm and stress, of alliteration, image, and ambiguity in the writing of a tragedy serves to reveal an immediate content of sensory material and myth, of memory and imagination. In such revelation this content emerges as held within form, as intuitive and absolute. It is the function of these elementary forms to achieve this disclosure. But more complex form not only reveals content, it catches and holds an initially fugitive content. The function of such form, of which tragedy is an example, thus may be thought of as the function of a path; a path which begins with the fugitive disclosure of content, and which is followed to make this content continuously accessible.

This movement along a path through the art-work allows the given to emerge through the forming activities of the artist or appreciator; to be articulated by form; to be a given part of an ultimate sustained aesthetic occasion. This fugitive aesthetic occasion is a movement from the opaque immediacy of the given toward articulated content, and a return to immediacy in immanent form. It is a movement of disclosure and reaffirmation of immediacy, a movement forth and back. But more than this, such an evocation of content through the forming movements in tragedy suggests the possibility of a continuing contribution to the aesthetic occasion by what is given. And it is just here that we may see the birth of tragedy, for what the form of tragedy does is to make the expression of this possibility of continuing contribution to disclosure of content by the given an explicit part of the art-work.

There are always nonhuman, given elements contributing to the development of any art-work. The givenness of sensuous materials or the uncanny figures and episodes in myth occur in art as yielding to the elementary kinds of forming we have discussed, and so as taking a place within the aesthetic occasion. In developing the form of tragedy, however, the artist introduces such given elements by emphasizing ways in which they evoke terror and horror. He presents the nonhuman as what opposes man, as alien.

157

By doing this he places the chief protagonist in a threatened position. The hero must move in response to what is negative, and in his response he inevitably penetrates to the limits of his nature; for the terrible circumstances which confront him permit of no specific resolution. Through the development of this movement the artist depicts a confrontation by what is other than man. In order to express the absoluteness of this confrontation the artist shows it as determined by man's bounded nature; that is, the hero not only cannot transcend his human limits and avoid destruction, but his fundamental nature requires him to *face* destruction. As developed in an art-work, heroic action expresses both man's need to be related to what is other than he, and his right to be human in this relation.

The movement which forms a tragedy takes the other which has been caught momentarily in the fugitive disclosure of content in the art-work—as, for example, sense material and myth—and recasts it to set it apart again as negative, as opposed to man. The tension introduced in this way is resolved by the heroic movement; but it is resolved only to express the possibility that the yielding to forming by the other, which has occurred in the case of sensory material and myth may be continued; that the other can be a continuing support of an aesthetic occasion, a contributor to its becoming. The forming which builds a tragedy destroys the image of man for the sake of expressing the possibility of the becoming of an aesthetic occasion through its incorporation of what is other than man. Yet, since man participates in an aesthetic occasion which has such a contribution, as the forming of the given through the elementary patterning of words and rhythms, for example, attests, we may believe still that it is only man's image which is destroyed and that he is in reality open. Phèdre's love which has become all-consuming passion destroys her individuality, but the creation of the drama returns her elemental need, her striving, to the flow of that process which is the aesthetic occasion. The hero symbolizes man's involvement in a process dominated by what is alien to him; and tragedy as art captures and presents a sense of what it means for man to accept the contribution of what is other than he to support a process of coming into being which is ultimate.

In tragedy what is other than man is seen as a continuing contributor to the coming into being which is an aesthetic occasion; the other is understood as supporting the continuing possibility of this becoming. Those modern artists who emphasize misery and suffering in the heroic movement need not miss this insight, whatever their final achievements. It is possible for such an artist to miss the tragic insight through emphasis upon those negative elements; but it is equally possible to miss this insight through a portrayal of the hero as noble. When the artist presents the hero as unequivocally a representative of a transcendent realm, his destruction loses its tragic quality. And if the artist presents the hero as merely a pathetic specimen of ordinary humanity, living his life and dying within the natural and social world, the sense of tragedy also vanishes.

The reason for an artist's failure to achieve tragedy in these two quite different ways seems the same. In both cases the significance of the heroic movement is located within the representation of drama; that is, in the one case in an account of a noble creature dwelling in a transcendent realm, and in the other case in an account of a pitiable personality in the environmental circumstances which determine him. Neither the portrayal of the hero as glorious nor as pathetic will do. Either portrayal requires a response from us which carries us out of the developing art-work. The point is not that glorious figures and pathetic figures have no place in art, for they may have; the point is that such figures, expressive as they are of human meanings and value, cannot stand as the culmination of the heroic movement. That movement begins in a conflict between man and what is alien to him, it develops this opposition, and its significance as an essential form in tragedy depends upon this. To resolve the opposition in the heroic movement by presenting the hero at the last as a figure having predominantly human meaning, whether of pathos or of glory, changes the structure of the drama.

Those modern artists who emphasize misery and suffering in the development of the heroic movement fail to achieve tragedy if they allow the sufferings of the hero to deny his expression of his right to be human, his right to stand in opposition to the alien he needs and that he seeks to confront. This right is lost if the hero becomes a pathetic and merely pitiable object; but it is not lost just because the heroic movement is outlined in terms of unrelieved suffering, or of the destruction of a soul. Even in *A Farewell to Arms*, after the pathetic death of Catherine, after the hero has told us:

> But after I had got them out and shut the door and turned off the light it wasn't any good. It was like saying good-by

to a statue. After a while I went out and left the hospital and walked back to the hotel in the rain.

and after such a restatement of the theme of the novel as:

The world . . . kills the very good and the very gentle and the very brave impartially. If you are none of these you can be sure it will kill you too but there will be no special hurry . . .

we still know that this explicit destruction is not the full story, for the very structure of the novel implies that after the narrator walked back to his hotel in the rain he wrote this novel. By this means he returned his own humanity, his love and Catherine's love to an art-work in which what is other than man is a contributor to an aesthetic occasion. The use of the first person narration here makes sure that however pitiable the end, we must see this end as the beginning and continuation of art.

Depiction of unrelieved suffering need not undermine the hero's right to stand opposed to the alien, so long as the artist depicts the hero's movement as a path through an art-work into an aesthetic occasion. How this is done and how well it is done is a problem for the artist's inventive genius; but when it is done we see beyond our pity for the human sufferer, beyond our terror of the alien circumstances which destroy him, and into the possibility of a continuing disclosure of content in which what is other than man is incorporated.

CHAPTER 6

HORIZONAL FORM: THE SUBLIME

I. Beauty

Euripides, in his drama *The Trojan Women*, depicts the confrontation by the women of Troy of the circumstances which engulf them. This play has been called the longest lament in existence. That is, this confrontation is presented as absolute, and it seems to have been Euripides' intention to avoid qualifying it or developing it in any way. It has been said that the play begins at the pitch of a high scream, and that the dramatic action continues at just this intensity without remission until the end. This is probably correct. There seems to be no development of any kind. A person viewing the play, or even the director of a performance, however, is tempted almost beyond resistance to see in the events of the drama a directed movement of some sort. For example, one may read into the death of Hector's son an intensification and culmination of the tragic destruction of the Trojan people; for in his death one may see the denial of the possibility of rebirth for Troy. And, having interpolated a culminating movement, one may also find an implied resolution. Perhaps, one may say, the closing scene suggests the death of the East and the birth of the West; so that the Trojan women, carried off from Troy as slaves, are to play a part in the birth of a new culture.

The temptation to interpolate a resolution has a part of its source in the sharpness with which Euripides develops the confrontation of the women of Troy by those alien forces which engulf them. The sharpness of this confrontation has the effect of stripping away recognizable patterns and traits which characterize the alien, so that what was initially simply the might of Greek arms becomes the other. The development of a reference to the other as opaque not only increases the sense of confrontation, but it also provides a locus within which a place for the women of Troy is imaginable. The opacity of the other makes resolution imaginable, and this is the ground for the temptation we have just noted.

When such imaginative interpolation on the part of the appreciator clearly goes beyond the intention of the artist it should be held in check; but it is quite possible for the artist himself to make use of the possibilities for resolution opened by development of a reference to the other. We may see this in the case of both comedy and tragedy. In a comedy negative elements are brought into an art-work and held there in such a way as to call for an acceptance by man of what falls outside human meaning and life. Here the role and character of the chief protagonist, the fool, may be developed to represent the acceptance by man of what is alien. Further, the more the distinction between man and what is alien to him is emphasized, the more the alien is presented as the other, and as opaque. In consequence of this opacity the artist may represent the fool, as he accepts the other, as coming to stand upon the threshold of a world in which he has a place. The imaginative suggestion is that the transfiguration of the fool places him in this world where the patterns and meanings of human life are related in some way to what is other than these. The resolution of the opposition is conceivable just because the alien term of the opposition remains unspecified.

This suggestion of a world in which a hero comes to stand is even more readily adjoined to tragedy, for here the emergence of the hero is always dependent upon a strong statement of the opposition between man and the alien. The development of this opposition requires that the configuration of the alien be left opaque. Further, in tragedy the hero is central to the action and, in the end, is put to the impossible task of living his acceptance of the alien. As the hero of a tragedy he stands upon the threshold of the alien and must cross this threshold and die. Yet his character is often so grand at the time of his death, that the circumstances of this death may call for a life beyond the opposition which destroys him, a life to be lived somehow in a land where this opposition is overcome. In tragedy, as in comedy, the incorporation of the hero in a world relating man and what opposes him can be imagined as taking place within an undefined scope.

The artists of comedy and tragedy who develop a reference to the other in this way often enough relate the hero to it by suggesting that he has a place in an ideal world framed within its undefined limits. To do this they may introduce references to God or the gods, to progress, or to larger wholes. In doing this they go beyond the limits of tragedy and comedy in the strict sense; for they suggest not merely man's recognition of what is other than himself as serving the disclosure of content, but his positive relation to the other. The significance of such references, of course, is to intimate that the opposition and conflict which occur on the level of the represented comic or tragic action need not be thought of as conflict on an ideal level. The terms of such references serve the artist, first of all, as means of contact with his audience. If he is to suggest to his audience the positive relation of man to the other, he needs to use the current versions of concepts of reconciliation and resolution, that is, concepts found in the dominant religious and philosophical orientations of his culture. When Sophocles places Oedipus in the sacred wood of the Furies at Colonus, we may understand him as doing this in order to convey to his Greek audience the sense of Oedipus incarnate, in terms close to their ordinary comprehension. And if O'Neill, in *Desire Under the Elms*, presents the pattern of the love between the wife and her stepson so that this *pair* is transfigured, we must see this as a style addressed to a modern audience for whom reconciliation and relation are most readily grasped in human terms. In general, symbols in art are not to be taken literally, and it seems fairly evident that symbols of the sort in question, God or the gods, progress, and larger wholes, are no exceptions. Reference in art to such ideal elements is not to be understood as suggesting a literal domain of reconciliation but as modifying in a special way the mode of participation of man and the other in an aesthetic occasion.

The movement in tragedy, which develops the hero to stand as man in opposition to what is other than man, carries beyond his death in the growth of the art-work and to the disclosure of content which is then seen to involve participation by the other. But the development of the art-work, taking place in this way, also involves a relation of the hero to the other; for it is through the development of the human nature of the hero and his death that what is other than man is brought to awareness as participating in an aesthetic occasion. It is this positive relation of man and the other which is symbolized, for example, in the transfiguration of the hero, in references to gods, and in suggestions of a place in which the hero might still live. The artist who develops this relation surely evokes an additional characterization of the aesthetic occasion. Of course, he introduces these symbols themselves into the art-work; but more than that, as we have noted, the intensity and impact of the aesthetic occasion is enhanced. In recognition of this enhanced quality it is often suggested that the development of this relation is a mounting of the ladder of beauty, a progression from easy through difficult beauty to the sublime.

To speak of a hierarchy of beauty, of degrees of beauty, is to suggest a progression of more and more inclusive forms which incorporate more and more recalcitrant elements into the art-work. Thus we may understand the artist as striving for greater beauty by introducing complexity and intricacy to the extent that this is done in Dante's *Inferno,* or even more so; by widening the scope of the subject matter included until he rivals the materials of Aristophanes and Rabelais, and stops at nothing; by incorporating situations as in the greatest tragedies where denial of hope and death reign unrelieved. A higher degree of beauty would be achieved when the almost overpowering richness of Dante's imagery is held for us in the power of aesthetic form; when the ribaldry of Rabelais' comedy is grasped in the net of human language and humane vision; when the triumph of death is a moment in the structure of a drama; when, that is, the artist is able to evoke the form which can hold more elements within it, regardless of what they are.

On this view, beyond the last rung of this ladder of forms would be found the highest degree of beauty, the sublime. There the artist stands confronting elements before which human vision falters, but in the face of which he is still able to evoke a sense of movement directed toward a form through which they could be given human meaning, which would contain both these elements and the artist. In this ultimate situation the artist (and later the appreciator) stands as part of the whole which this adumbrated form defines in principle. In the artist's aspiring movement toward participation in this whole, he seems to catch sight of the way in which man and what is other than man are ultimately related, the way they ultimately participate in the unity of an aesthetic occasion.

From this standpoint beauty marks that process which brings the artist, and later the appreciator, into an ascending order of more and more encompassing relation with what is alien to him. And degrees of beauty reflect this hierarchy, with the highest degree of beauty being called the sublime. A part of the plausibility of this account lies in its mirroring of the significance ordinarily thought to reside in those symbols which the artist often uses to suggest the sublime: God or the gods, progress, or an ideal whole. The difficulty of this account is that it makes of all beauty only an anticipation of the final relation of man to what is other than himself. Thus even the purest and the simplest beauty must be understood as a quality of movement beyond whatever perfection seems to have been attained. It seems simpler and closer to the truth to let the word beauty signify the quality of an aesthetic occasion as fugitive, as an initial disclosure of content which, though transient, is absolute. By the same token we should let the word sublime signify the quality of that moment in which man and what is other than himself come to sustaining participation in the aesthetic occasion. This sustained occasion must reflect the absoluteness of beauty; but it is characterized by the transmutation and incorporation of man as evidenced in inception, presence, and renewal, and of the other as evidenced in that somewhat more opaque sustaining movement revealed in the comic, comedy of appearance, and tragedy. A sustained aesthetic occasion adds continuity to beauty, it provides the temporal overview afforded by a movement beginning in beauty and, taking the absoluteness of beauty as a standard, maintaining it as well. It is from this perspective that beauty appears as ephemeral, as fugitive. Yet, still, it appears as the origin of a movement sustaining it.

Beauty, then, is a quality of what seems to be a fugitive disclosure of content, within which man stands accidentally and to some extent in spite of himself, as participant in an ultimate process. Here there is no standard outside this movement; here, in the moment, the miraculous revealing of content comprises whatever goals there are. In this moment human questions are silenced and human questing stilled. Here there is a fugitive disclosure which is perfection. The absoluteness which beauty evidences attests the ultimate bounding moment of creation itself.

II. *The Sublime*

The moment of beauty needs no apology, and indeed none is possible. Once having stood within this fugitive disclosure, man must take it as the standard, seeking to walk that path which leads to it, endeavoring to return to it when somehow he falls out of its magic circle.

If beauty—which is a quality of a transient disclosure—does not vary, is absolute, it is still correct to say that some artists have a more profound vision than others, that their participation in the process disclosing content is deeper. The talented artist, the great artist, participates in an initial disclosure of content, and the beauty which is the quality of this moment is absolute (as it is, also, for the lesser artist). All artists go to the original spring and bring back the same water. Yet the receptacle of the great artist is different, and the purity and flavor of the water are better preserved by him. He is more aware that an initial disclosure of content occurs in the distinction and relation of a process of forming and an opaque given; he is more aware, that is, that beauty has no designatable sources, that whatever process of forming there is and whatever is given are held entirely within the fugitive moment of disclosure. Thus the greater artist apprehends more clearly the nature of the standard of beauty to which he is committed, that *it is its own sign*, that it cannot be referred to any source.

In consequence such an artist strives to relate his own artistic activities, his values, and his nature to the process we have called disclosure of content, and in such a profound way that there is no residue. The more talented artist loses himself more completely in the aesthetic occasion; he comes to stand, not as a contributor to it, but in contributions made; he is to be found, not as a single source, but as a metamorphosis of its patterns. In his handling of reflexive forms, such an artist reveals his intent to make of himself and man not a source of an aesthetic occasion, but a constituent and aspect of it, through contributions recognizing and sustaining the inherent absoluteness of beauty.

Similarly, the greater artist reflects in his handling of the materials and negative elements of his art—that which makes beauty a standard—the fact that it is its own sign. He develops the art-work to open to these fully, and to avoid their appearing as particular sources. He elaborates the acceptance of the other as participating in an aesthetic occasion, suggesting that it sustains beauty, that it comes to stand, not as a source or contributor, but in integral contributions. In his handling of transcendental forming, such an artist makes clear his concern that what is other than man should become an integral participant in the occasion. In the handling by the great artist, comedy and tragedy show that what is other than man is found not so much as a source of this art, not so much as the recalcitrant raw materials, say of language, character, situation, and history, not so much as that terrible circumstance which confronts the hero; but as a sustaining participant in beauty, as manifested in the continuous process of a sustained aesthetic occasion.

In guiding his artistic activities and in handling the other, an intent of the artist is to avoid a result in which he and the other stand outside the dynamic circle of an aesthetic occasion, and so are to be understood as contributors to, as sources of it. The greater artist is more effective in carrying through this intent; it is something he does by means of the development of reflexive and transcendental forms. Yet if the characterization of beauty by inception, presence, and renewal suggests a movement incorporating man into the aesthetic occasion, then the more subtle this characterization the clearer it becomes that this sustaining movement is distinct from the very similar movement suggested by the characterization of beauty through the comic, comedy of appearance, and tragedy. Indeed, the more fully the movement incorporating man is developed, the more evidently does this diverge from the sustaining movement incorporating the other. The greater artist discovers, as in tragedy, a fundamental opposition between these movements, an opposition which suggests irreducibly different sources.

In the work of the greater artist this opposition is developed most profoundly in order to prepare for its resolution. And in the work of such an artist this opposition, sharply stated, is overcome by what we call *horizonal form*, a forming activity introduced into the art-work for this purpose. The central function of horizonal form is to accord explicit recognition to the absoluteness of beauty, a recognition which can be achieved only by overcoming that apparent opposition of man and the other implicit in the reflexive and transcendental forming entering into a sustained aesthetic occasion. Horizonal forming is introduced into the art-work, often, by referring the movement of inception, presence, and renewal *and* the sustaining movement of transcendental forming, whose sharp difference suggests antithetical sources, to the infinite, or more exactly, to the boundless. Reference of these movements to the boundless stands in lieu of reference to a source, and, in fact, is a part of a pattern which explicitly denies the significance, with respect to a sustained aesthetic occasion, of any reference to a source.

Development of a reference to the boundless in an art-work makes explicit the artist's recognition of initially disclosed content as absolute, his concern for beauty in its own terms. It serves, also, as a step in taking the absoluteness of beauty as the standard guiding the way in which the artist and the other are incorporated and transmuted in an aesthetic occasion; that is, the way they come to be participant in this occasion and sustain it. It enables the artist to depict this participation in principle as a movement neither of inception, presence, and renewal nor of support by the other; but as a movement out of the boundless into a concrete unity, a bounded being; a movement which the artist may symbolize as an incarnation of a figure or figures at the level of represented action; and a movement which he may present as directed—a crystallization inherent in the art-work—into the bounded being of a sustained aesthetic occasion. Let us consider some examples of this bounding movement and the quality of sublimity which characterizes an aesthetic occasion in relation to it, before returning to its analysis.

The sublime is more commonly recognized, perhaps, in situations involving natural grandeur. We speak of seascapes as sublime, or we refer to the sublimity of the night sky. The extended masses of a towering mountain range often impress us as sublime. In these cases a not uncommon sense of the natural scene finds its detail as illustrative of infinite variety, boundlessness. The importance of this is fairly evident in the case of a natural landscape, for we may note that if we are so close as to be a part of the landscape, we apprehend this part in specific detail and lose the sense of the sublimity of the scene. We experience the same loss

173

if we are far from the scene, say miles across the plain, for then we apprehend the structural patterns of the whole. In either case, the context of the boundless as infinite variety, to which we otherwise might refer the details of the scene, disappears as our nearness or great distance permits a completely determinate grasp of the parts or whole of the landscape.

The sublimity of a natural scene, however, involves not only a response to its illustration of infinite variegation, but a positive response as well. Despite our inability to determine the night sky completely, we are not baffled by its myriad stars and limitless extent. We realize that the sky extends beyond our powers of dealing with it; yet we accept the accidental character of the constellations we arrange upon its velvet infinity. This sense of infinity does not prevent us from seeing Orion or the Pleiades in the heavens; but we see them there as efflorescent rather than as determinate forms. Their patterns emerge. This sense of the disclosing of content in relation to the unbounded as infinitely various is often characteristic of the situations in which the quality of the sublime occurs. In natural situations where this happens the limitless sensuous immediacy of, say, the night sky does not fix the elements it holds. We are not aware of its velvet blackness as determining the natures and outlines of those patterned elements which are disclosed in it. Rather, we are aware of a movement from the boundless as indeterminate on the one hand, into limited and bounded disclosure on the other. It is not the immediacy of the texture of the night sky which serves, in our awareness, as the referent for the constellations of the stars displayed within it. The referent is the boundlessness or potential richness of this sky.

In such a reference the limited patterns of the constellations are grasped as an aspect of a movement in which the specific constellations crystallize out of the indeterminate, a movement which reveals what is bounded *in itself*. When this happens the quality of the sublime characterizes the movement and suffuses the bounded disclosure. This suffusion is even more evident in natural situations involving limitless power, such as a raging sea, a storm, or a waterfall, which often impress us as sublime. Indeed, any situation in which overwhelming power is evidenced may impress us in this way. That which can overpower us, that against which we cannot stand, sharply limns the bounds of our being, and yet singles us out, limited as we are, as the harbingers of beauty. Thus, relative to overwhelming power, the emergence into presence of our own limited natures suggests that those things which are driven over the raging waters or tossed upon the violent winds of a storm, are participants in the absoluteness of the aesthetic occasion as well.

Through selective emphasis upon aspects of a situation, the creative artist can also present limited patterns as crystallizing out of the boundless. In a typical Hindu temple the architects have intended to reflect the extent and variety of human life in the specific details of the sculpture and relief which cover its walls. The sculpture and relief constitute a depiction of individual and collective human life and history in concrete detail. However, concrete as this depiction is, it is not simply an account of human life, for it refers in this context not only to what happens to man, but to the interior volumes of the temple, which contain the central figure of the lingam symbolizing the awe-inspiring forces of creation. The depiction of life and history is not merely representative. It refers also to the awful power of creation, a power which is presented as indeterminate and overwhelming by the complex interrelation of darkened interior volumes and the opaque centrality of the lingam itself. In consequence, human life as depicted is presented as attuned to the forces of creation. These forces are suggested in the movement disclosing human life emerging out of an underlying indeterminate and opaque flux. The elements of human life and history are not presented as products of a causal sequence; they stand as individualized, as disclosed in and through their relation to the dark flow of creation.

In much Hindu religious art an effort is made to state and develop the nature of this reference more sharply than can be done in a temple. Let us consider two examples illustrating this emphasis. The first is the statue of the Siva-Trinity in the caves at Elephanta north of Bombay. Over the right shoulder, growing out of the central form of the statue, is the male profile of Siva, suggesting virility, will-power, defiance, haughtiness, valor, and temper; even cruelty. Over the left shoulder of the central form is another profile of Siva which might be called feminine; it suggests the seductive power of nature, blossom and fruit, gentle charm, sweetness. These two profiles we see as in conflict; indeed, their antagonism is explicitly stated in the statue.

No doubt we are right if we understand the conflict to be

between the cruel force of creation and its beneficent fertility. In an art-work developing on the basis of the statue we may sense a resolution of this conflict. In part, the resolution is brought about because the statue is hewn from the living rock of the cave, so that its texture and material leads us back into the bowels of the earth. And since the matrix out of which the statue emerges includes those dark recesses where the openness of space disappears into the amorphousness of matter, content is disclosed with reference to the indeterminateness and awful power of the internal creative forces of the earth itself. This reference is developed in a special way here in the central face of the god. Here Siva is presented as aloof and silent, majestic and inscrutable. This central face is lofty and indifferent, august and immovable; in it the god looks out as the incarnation of the limitlessness and overwhelming power of creation, as testimony that creation is to be found immanent in the limited patterns and individual details of its manifestations. The central face dominates the two profiles, holding them together without incorporating them within meaningful form, as the evidence of a movement of incarnation which brings the ultimacy of creation into its manifestations. The central face repeats the indeterminateness and power of the creative forces of the cosmos in a bounded but not determinate way.

The complex aesthetic form incorporating such an incarnation appears even more clearly in a second example from Hindu religious art, in the statue of the dancing god, the Siva-Nataraja, versions of which are to be found all over India. In this statue the upper of the two right hands of the god holds a small drum, shaped like an hour-glass, which is often used for beating out a rhythm. Since in India sound is associated with ether, the first of the five elements, out of which the other four (air, fire, water, earth) unfold, the drum suggests the creative moments of cosmic evolution. The upper of the two left hands of the god, by contrast, bears in its palm a flame. Fire is the traditional element of destruction, and the element which destroys the whole world at the close of each course of those epochs which make up world history in this instance. The statue thus represents the conflict of fertility and destruction, the coursing of events in their flowering and withering: fire stands as that which annihilates and opposes the sound which creates. But this is not the ultimate message of the statue.

The second right hand of the god gives the "fear not" gesture, suggesting, despite the conflict of creation and destruction, both protection and peace. The second left hand is extended in a gesture miming the outstretched trunk of the elephant, the remover of obstacles. This hand points to the left foot of the god, the foot which often signifies release from the toils of appearance. The right foot of the god rests, in many versions of the statue, upon the prostrate body of a demon, Apasmara Purusha. This is the demon of heedlessness, the demon who holds man within the boundaries of appearance, who symbolizes the blindness of the forces expressed overtly in human life. Here this demon is represented as conquered. But how has he been conquered?

The patterns of the statue suggest to an appreciator that one of the conditions of conquering that blindness in which attention is focused upon appearance only, is an invocation of the deep meanings of myth, in this case the Hindu myth. In this myth the drum evokes the rich but inscrutable sound of the universe, the very heartbeat of creation, and also all the magical forms of speech, the incantations, which lead to the revelation of the mysteries of creation. And in this myth the fire evokes the overwhelming power against which no creature can stand, but the raging force of which is somehow essential to the emergence of creatures in the flow of creation. The reference to myth in the statue shifts the focus of attention from the analytical details of cosmic evolution, to the potentiality of this process for infinite variety and to the infinite power which is implicit in it.

The patterns of the statue suggest more than this shift of attention to the perspective afforded by reference to the boundless—they suggest as well a new way in which the details of the cosmic evolution can be grasped from this perspective. The statue is the figure of a dancing god, caught in an instant of time. But the statue is tilted slightly out of the vertical plane; and, in consequence, in the artwork developed in response to the statue, the movement of the dance begins. Each of the gestures of the dance found in the movements of the arms and legs represents different and opposing aspects of the flow of creation. These gestures run through a variety of meanings which conflict in their concrete detail, but in the sequence of the choreography these meanings emerge in relation to a potentiality for infinite variety manifested through infinite force. The dancing god is held in a ring of flames, which is to be understood as the incarnation of the raging fire which illumines and inspires his movements. Despite the frenzied movements of the dance, the face of the god remains aloof and impassive. Siva-Nataraja is not merely a creature having a place in the sequence of time; he is an incarnation who holds within himself the complexities, the antagonisms, the potentialities, and the force of the creative flow itself; he is a bounded being who is the incarnation of creation.

There are other and perhaps better examples of the quality of the sublime in art than those just given, such as the works of the four masters of the Yüan dynasty, or many of Van Gogh's works, to mention only paintings. In these other examples, however, the reference to the boundless is often much more complexly developed than in Hindu art; the central point is consequently more difficult to suggest. If Hindu art suggests the function of the boundless as an aspect of horizonal forming in the art-work, we have need to consider the nature and function of the boundless in contributing to such form in more technical detail and in a different context. There can be little doubt that when reference to overwhelming power or the indeterminate in a developing art-work includes a symbol of incarnation, the suggested bounded disclosure of content is characterized for artist and appreciator as having a singular intensity and impact. What is not so evident to reflection is the nature and significance of this intensity and impact.

The crystallization of the incarnate figure out of the boundless mirrors beauty, that fugitive disclosure of content which, having no specific origin, is absolute; but it mirrors as well the sustained disclosure of content as coalescing out of the streams of reflexive and transcendental forming which, whatever their differences, take this absoluteness as guiding the mode of their support. The incarnate figure mirrors the movements of this forming which sustains the aesthetic occasion; and which, as a movement of incorporation, comprises the aesthetic occasion as sustained.

In developing an art-work, the artist and the appreciator are aware of a moment of beauty. They are aware of this as an absolute but fugitive disclosure of content; and they are moved to relate to and sustain it. That this be possible, however, requires that their own natures be transmuted, that they come to stand not as specific sources of beauty, not as creators of it, but as contributions to its support. This is a requirement that whatever is essentially human be transmuted to support the ultimate process disclosing content, to be understood in relation to this process, and, ideally, as an element in it. Such a transmutation changes, for example, human meanings into contrasts and symbols used in the art-work to reflect the process disclosing content; a use which limns this process, this disclosure, giving to it a temporal pattern—an inception, a presence, and a renewal.

As this limning appears initially in comedy and tragedy, it constitutes a border beyond which what is other than man may be glimpsed, if not understood. No doubt the figure of the hero who stands opposed to the alien suggests the nature of this border; but the acceptance of what is other than man in comedy and tragedy also suggests that the incorporation of the other into the aesthetic occasion makes the limning of this process involving man not a line marking off human contributions from the other, but a characterization of the process as a movement in which both man and what is other than man are involved. Such limning bounds the process, it characterizes the movement as one which accords a horizon to the disclosure of content and to the aesthetic occasion.

The movements incorporating man and what is other than man into an aesthetic occasion may be seen to flow together. They are bounding movements, movements which inscribe the horizon of the aesthetic occasion. This horizon is a development of the patterns of inception, presence, and renewal which suggests that the aesthetic occasion is sustained by the incorporation of man into the process disclosing content, for the inner face of the horizon has the significance of permitting unrestricted articulation, unbroken space for the incorporation of meaning. But the horizon, on its outer face, as it were, extends the movements of transcendental forming toward what is other than man. It opens without restriction to incorporate the other into the aesthetic occasion, in recognition of its power to sustain. The horizon, affording space for unrestricted and extended development in these two ways, also cuts off any reference to external sources; its always closed bound reflects the absoluteness of beauty, and reaffirms and sustains this absoluteness. The horizon of a sustained aesthetic occasion attests the identification of its sustaining movements with that ultimate movement which has the quality of beauty, the ultimate movement of a fugitive disclosure of content. Such an identification is, of course, in part an identity of intent; but the possibility is genuine that the activities developing an art-work are one with that process which discloses content. This possibility is found in the bounding movement which develops the horizon of an aesthetic occasion, in the sustaining movement which expresses the continuity of man's and what is other than man's support in the articulate, open unity of the horizon. This movement, symbolized in art in the incarnate figure emerging from the boundless, is the ground for the intensity and impact of the sublime; for it attests that man can return to and contribute to that ultimate process from which he, also, sprang.

III. Man and Art

The realm of art is defined by the horizon of a sustained aesthetic occasion. An aesthetic occasion is an emergence, a disclosing of content evoked from an opaque given through a forming process within which man, as participant, happens to find himself. The realm of art is entered so soon as the fugitive character of such an occasion—that is, beauty—calls for and receives man's sustaining response. But such response may be, initially, so tentative and so undeveloped that its significance cannot be caught. The realm of art comes to flower when man's response is developed in reflexive and transcendental forming and made to serve the absoluteness of beauty. Then man participates in this realm.

From the perspective of man, participation in the realm of art suggests a harmony between himself and what is other than he, a harmony which is attested in the inscribing of the horizon of an aesthetic occasion. In this harmony man finds a way in which he might attain to perfection, and some evidence, at least, of the possibility of perfection. Beauty of itself intoxicates and arouses us; but that inscribing of the horizon which we sense as the sublime shows us that beauty is not only an accident. It shows us that our own creaturely natures, together with the natures of other creatures, can be returned to that process from which they came, so that our relations with this process can come to determine what they and we are. The sense of mystery associated with this return and determination is just the association of ourselves with what is absolute and the discovery that we, too, participate in and continue this. When we first hear the flow of this process in beauty, and when we listen to the sound and significance of the bounding movement of creation in the sublime, we sense the ground of all those efforts, strivings, and aspirations which lie just below the surface of the activities of our rational, moral, and practical natures. And if this ground, as we have seen, manifests itself more readily in the realm of art, this too, serves to support our hope that perfection is possible and may be attained in other realms as well.

APPENDIX

MANUSCRIPT DRAFT

The following is a transcript of the original draft of "The Tiger" from the Rossetti MS, Blake's changes being indicated typographically by placing them in consecutive order, one below another, deleted words or phrases being printed in italics. The manuscript is unpunctuated. The finished version is reproduced on p. 69.

THE TYGER

1   Tyger Tyger burning bright
    In the forests of the night
    What immortal hand & eye
                    or
    Could frame thy fearful symmetry
    Dare

2   In what distant deeps or skies
    Burnt in
    Burnt the fire of thine eyes
    The cruel
    On what wings dare he aspire
    What the hand dare seize the fire

3   And what shoulder & what art
    Could twist the sinews of thy heart
    And when thy heart began to beat
    What dread hand & what dread feet

    Could fetch it from the furnace deep
    And in thy horrid ribs dare steep
    In the well of sanguine woe
    In what clay & in what mould
    Were thy eyes of fury rolld

4   What the hammer   what the chain
    Where   *where*

In what furnace was thy brain
What the anvil   What *the arm*
                              arm
                              grasp
                              clasp
                    dread grasp
Could its deadly terrors *clasp*
Dare   *grasp*
                      clasp

6   Tyger Tyger burning bright
    In the forests of the night
    What immortal hand & eye
    Dare *form* thy fearful symmetry
          frame

    [On the opposite page of the MS]
    Burnt in distant deeps or skies
    The cruel fire of thine eyes
    Could heart descend or wings aspire
    what the hand dare seize the fire

5   (3) And *did he laugh* his work to see
              dare he *smile*
                    laugh
              W*hat the shoulder*   *what the knee*
                    ankle
    (4) Did he who made the lamb make thee
        Dare
    (1) When the stars threw down their spears
    (2) And waterd heaven with their tears

INDEX

Absolute: 36, 172, 182, 183 ff.
Action: 19 ff., 25 ff., 30, 33 ff.,
    40, 90, 141 ff.
Action Painting: 25 ff.
Adams, Henry: 134
  –*Autobiography*, 134, 137
Aesthetic   Occasion: 36 ff.,
    38 ff., 43 ff., 56, 61, 68,
    77, 85 ff., 102 ff., 128,
    135, 137, 157 ff., 166 ff.,
    171 ff., 181 ff.
Aesthetic Response:
  –and beauty, 170–2
  –and creativity, 81–90
  –and forming, 3, 6–7, 47–9
  –and inception, 58
  –and   negative   elements,
    102–6
  –and ordinary response, 6,
    11, 17–24
  –as participation, 38, 62–3,
    89 ff., 181 ff.
  –and presence, 78
  –and   receptivity, openness,
    89–93, 111, 114–5, 121–
    3, 128–9, 150
  –and reflexive forms, 62–3
  –and the sublime, 172–5,
    183–4
  –and tragedy, 134–7, 157–
    61
Aesthetic Vision: 3 ff., 10 ff.,
    17 ff.
Alien: v. Other
Amphitryon: 15
Appreciator: 30–2
Architecture: 53, 58–9, 78, 80,
    83–4, 86–9, 175–6

Aristophanes: 167
Aristotle: 31, 140
Art Forms: 54, 78 ff., 88–9,
    93
Artist—*See* Aesthetic Response
Art-Object: 10 ff., 30, 33, 79
Art-Work: 25 ff., 31 ff., 39,
    55, 90 ff., 103 ff., 129,
    157 ff., 171 ff.
Autobiography: 134–5, 137

Basho: 12
Beauty: 163 ff., 167 ff., 170 ff.,
    180 ff.
Beethoven: 64
Bergson: 31
Blake: 12, 19, 68, 103
Botticelli: 13
Bounded: 68, 91 ff., 144, 148,
    173, 182, 184
Boundless: 172 ff.
Brecht: 95, 96

Caricature: 111 ff.
Cellini: 51
Ceramics: 44–9, 57
Chaplin: 120 ff.
  –early comedies, 120 ff.
Chartres: 58, 50
Cinema: 120–3
Comedy: 95 ff.
Comedy   of   Appearance:
    120 ff., 123
Comic: 106 ff.
Content—*See* Disclosed Con-
    tent

187

Contrast: forming by, 59
Creation: 169, 183–4
  –as creativity—*See* Aesthetic Response
  –in Blake, 68 ff.

Dante: 167
Degrees of Beauty: 167
Disclosed Content: 23, 27 ff., 31, 35 ff., 38 ff., 43 ff., 56, 58 ff., 67, 77, 88 ff., 98, 102, 105, 129, 137, 156 ff., 168 ff., 173, 180 ff.
Drama: 4, 15–7, 54, 57, 78, 109, 111, 124–9, 139, 140–61, 163–4, 166, 181

Eichendorf: 111
Eliot, Thomas Stearns: 151
Euripedes: 163
Evil: 95 ff.; *see also* Transcendental Forms
Expressive elements: 25 ff.; *see also* Reflexive Forms

Farewell to Arms: 139, 151, 160–1
Fate; in tragedy, 138 ff.
Figure: 42 ff.
Flaubert: 138
Flaw, tragic: 143 ff., 148
Folktales: 100, 116–7
Fool; in comedy, 120 ff., 131, 164
Form (Forming): *See* Aesthetic Response
Formed-content: 33 ff.; *see also* Disclosed Content
Function: *see* Inception *and* Modern Architecture

Giraudoux: 15
Given: 22 ff., 41, 110, 158; *see also* Other
Goethe: 143
Grimm: 99
Grosz: 41

Hamlet: 146 ff., 150, 151
Hathaway: 117
Haydn: 34
Hegel: 31
Hemingway: 139
Henri: 33
Hero: 131 ff.
  –fate of, 138 ff.
  –heroic movement, 151 ff.
  –transfiguration of, 152, 163 ff.
Hoffman, Hans: 25
Homer: 7
Hopkins: 13, 20
Horizonal form: 172 ff., 182, 183
Human nature: *See* Participation
Humor, frontier: 115 ff.

Ibsen: 140
Ideal elements: 165–7
Illusion: *See* Ordinary Experience *and* Comedy of Appearance
Incarnation: 173 ff., 177, 180, 183
Inception: 61 ff.
Intuition: 20–3, 38; *see also* Disclosed Content *and* Aesthetic Occasion

Jazz: 32
Joyce: 152

Kandinski: 23
Keats: 18, 19
Kinaesthesis: 40
Klee: 29, 30, 40
deKooning: 25

Laughter: 108 ff.
Levine: 113–4
Line: 40–2

Malkin: 74
Mann: 89, 141
Marin: 27
Markandeya: 100, 101
"The Mask of Evil": 95 ff.
Mathieu: 29
Melville: 98 ff., 133
Merzbau: 29
Milton: 151
Modern architecture: 59, 86 ff.
Molière: 15
Music: 23, 34, 36, 41–2, 51,
    53, 64–8, 79, 81–2
"Myth of Markandeya:"
    101 ff.

Nature: 173–5
Negative elements: 95 ff.
Nietzsche: 11
Novel: 34, 54, 63–4, 83, 89,
    98–100, 118–9, 133, 139,
    141, 153, 161, 167

Oedipus the King: 144 ff.
O'Neill: 124 ff., 143, 166
Openness: see Aesthetic Re-
    sponse, Comedy, Comedy
    of Appearance, Comic,
    and Tragedy
Ordinary Experience: 3 ff.,
    38–9

Ordinary Experience (con-
    tinued)
–destruction of, 10 ff., 18
–emotional, 6, 35
–intellectual, 4, 35
–moral, 7, 35
–practical, 6, 9, 35
Other (Alien): 105 ff., 114,
    122 ff., 131 ff., 150, 158,
    161, 163 ff., 183

Pain: 104
Painting: 13, 22–3, 25 ff., 33–
    4, 36, 40–1, 43–4, 51,
    78–81, 113–4
Parody: 111 ff.
Pattern: See Symmetry
Picasso: 29, 34
Pleasure (in Comedy): 106 ff.
Po Chü-i: 136
–"Last Poem," 136, 137
Poe: 28, 29, 30
Poetry: 11–3, 21, 39, 51, 53,
    68–78, 83, 95–6, 133,
    136–7, 167, 187–8
Prelude in C sharp minor: 66
Presence: 67, 78
Presented Value: 51 ff.

Rabelais: 167
Rachmaninoff: 66
Racine: 153
Realm of Art: 9–10, 48, 88,
    93, 183 ff.
Reflexive Form: 51 ff., 62–3,
    171, 172, 182
Rembrandt: 34
Renewal: 86 ff., 93, 182
Representation: 51, 63 ff.
Rimbaud: 18
Rockefeller: 57
Rospiglioso Cup: 51 ff., 55

Sculpture: 51–2, 55, 60, 78–9, 176–81
Sensation: 19–22
Shakespeare: 111, 142, 146 ff., 155
Sibelius: 34
Siva-Nataraja: 177 ff.
Siva Trinity: 176 ff.
Sophocles: 54, 144 ff., 151, 166
Space: 33–4
Strange Interlude: 124 ff.
Strauss: 65
Sublime: 168, 169 ff.
Sullivan: 86
Sumiye: 27
Symbols: 68, 77
Symmetry: 42 ff.

"The Tiger": 68 ff
  –Manuscript Draft, 187–88
Time: 29, 33–4

Tinguely: 25
Tolstoi: 6, 54
Tragedy: 131 ff.
Tragic Flaw: 143 ff., 148
Transcendental Form: 95 ff., 129 ff., 171, 172, 182
Twain: 110, 118 ff.
Typee: 98 ff.

Ultimate, process as: 169, 183
Ugly: 104

Van Gogh: 13, 180
Von Kleist: 15
Waley: 136
Whitman: 21, 133
Widener: 57
Wright: 86, 87

Yeats: 18